THE COMPLETE GUNDOG

John Paley

THE COMPLETE GUNDOG

Compiled by

John Humphreys

David & Charles
Newton Abbot London

BY THE SAME AUTHOR

Living Off the Land
Hides, Calls and Decoys
The Sportsman Head to Toe
Modern Pigeon Shooting
Stanley Duncan, Wildfowler
The Shooting Handbook (Ed)
 1983–1987

The Do-It-Yourself-Gameshoot
Learning to Shoot
The Woods Belong to Me (Ed)
Hunter's Fen
Shooting Pigeons
The Country Sportsman's Record Book
 & Journal

Ilustrations by
 John Paley
 Dave Parfitt
 John Barnard
 The contributors

British Library Cataloguing in Publication Data

Humphreys, John, *1939–*
 The complete gundog.
 1. Gundogs
 I. Title
 636.752

 ISBN 0–7153–9412–6

Printed in Great Britain by
The Bath Press   Bath   Avon
for David & Charles Publishers plc
Brunel House   Newton Abbot   Devon

Contents

DAVID & CHARLES FIELDSPORTS AND FISHING TITLES

Introduction

This book concerns itself with the training of dogs for the gun. Many and varied are the breeds available which man has pressed into service for this ancient task. Bred carefully and their natural instincts finely honed to hunt, flush, retrieve, pick up the slightest whiff of game scent, these dogs will work in water, snow and the harshest conditions of the European winter and still remain loving, faithful companions and members of the family.

It is a book unlike any other, for while there have been a number of excellent works devoted to this noble art, each has, as a rule, been written by one person. No single trainer, no matter how great the depth of his or her expertise and experience is able to write authoritatively on every single branch of training and of every breed. In this book is assembled a 1st XI (and a twelfth man) of some of the best writers and dog-trainers in the British Isles. Each has taken a single aspect of training and field work and devoted a chapter solely to that. Each could have contributed in other ways, but for one writer to apply the microscope of his or her knowledge to one element, allows this book to cover areas upon which some others have but touched.

The distinguished team of contributors have each been given free rein and it may be that some of their observations overlap, some might even be contradictory, but they each add a piece to the jigsaw and prove, in doing so, that the last section will surely never be fitted into place and that even the best of us is learning all the time. Such is part of the beauty of the game.

It is inconceivable that the modern shooting man should pursue his sport without his dog, or at least without a dog present. Quite apart from the element of companionship, a bird has only to drop out of sight in thick cover, over an unjumpable ditch, in a river or on a lake or to fall wounded and run many hundreds of yards to shelter and be lost where no human eye or ingenuity will recover it. Such is the height of irresponsibility. The general public is closely scrutinising the conduct of all field sports and the shooting man's house can be seen to be in order if he can show the world that his runners are retrieved and that he leaves no quarry species to lie and rot and thus be wasted, all for his lack of a dog.

Training dogs for the field has rarely been more popular nor its degree of expertise so advanced. Methods have changed much since the bad old days of the whip, when dogs were broken rather than moulded. The likes of the late Richard Sharpe broke that cruel practice half a century ago, since when dogs have been better trained, happier and have served their masters better.

I am by no means an expert, and my shooting friends will be relieved, but not surprised, to hear me make that disclaimer. Experienced, yes, for I have owned a great number of dogs since I was a youngster and have never been without my own labrador to accompany my shooting outings. Currently I have two, one old one on the point of retirement, and one youngster coming on. Each of my dogs has been different from the rest, many have been headstrong monsters which would win no competitions, although many a hard bird they have retrieved. The knack is still to be learnt but with each newcomer to my kennels, hope springs rekindled in my breast. This time, surely, I will get it right.

My own contribution to this book takes the form of a series of accounts of my experiences with seven of my dogs which have taught me most. They are held up to the reader not as models of how things should be done but of the trials and also the pleasures which await the new owner, of the glorious possibilities, of the pitfalls, the heartbreaks and moments of supreme joy which go with having your own gundog. The tales may teach by example and will serve to balance the wealth of expertise which surrounds them in these pages. My hope, and that of my friends who contributed to this book, is that our efforts will result in one or two shooting folk and triallers avoiding some of the obvious mistakes, encouraging them to press on and maybe opening their minds to some marvels and memorable experiences.

I am grateful to John Paley whose inimitable sketches enhance these pages, as I am to my old companion Dave Parfitt who has contributed many of the black-and-white photographs. Others have been provided by the various writers while the colour work is by a remarkable field-sports photographer from Scarborough, Jack Barnard. The pleasure he alone will gain from seeing his hitherto underexposed work in print will, in itself, be worth the time and effort involved.

John Humphreys
Bottisham, Easter 1989

Early Days

PETER MOXON

Peter Moxon acquired his interest in dogs and country pursuits during childhood in rural Kent. After recovering from a serious breakdown in health he set up gundog training kennels near Canterbury in 1942, and a year later became Kennel Editor of Shooting Times, *to which magazine he has contributed regularly to this day.*

In 1957 Peter bought a large kennels in Worcestershire, and for over twenty years was both a competitor and an A Panel judge at field trials, as well as reporting and photographing them and acting as instructor at training classes, of which he was a pioneer. His book Gundogs: Training & Field Trials, *published in 1952, has gone into fifteen editions and become a standard work on the subject, and his second book* Training the Roughshooter's Dog, *published in 1977, is now in its sixth edition. Although semi-retired, Peter continues his journalistic activities and interest in the gundog scene, and derives much satisfaction from the advice he is able to give novice owners and handlers both personally and in print, particularly on the psychological aspect of canine education.*

No matter which breed of gundog you have decided to invest in, it is vitally important and essential for success that you make a serious study of the subject and get yourself into the right frame of mind beforehand. Far too many folk plunge into ownership at the deep end and make all sorts of silly mistakes, quite possibly ruining the chance of a promising pupil for all time, by ignoring this dictum. Unfortunately, the average Britisher seems to be imbued with the idea that he knows 'all about dogs' almost from birth and, worse still, that dogs know all about *him* and understand exactly what he requires of them. Nothing could be further from the truth, as a lifetime spent among dogs and dog-owners has taught me. I offer no excuses for launching into a sermon on that most important of all aspects of canine ownership, psychology – both human and canine – in the hope that it may assist readers to avoid at least the majority of mistakes so commonly made by handlers (including myself) during their novice stage.

Psychology

The ideal relationship between man and dog must be built upon mutual understanding, trust and, probably above all, *respect*. This calls for great patience on the part of the handler who must, at the outset, get it firmly fixed

Hand signals should be perfectly clear

in his head that a dog does not possess the reasoning ability of a human, and frequently has to be shown what is required of him. The successful handler is the one who trains himself to endeavour to see things from the dog's point of view – what I term 'thinking like a dog' – and also does his level best to keep one jump ahead and anticipate his pupil's reactions. This may seem a daunting prospect but it isn't as bad as it sounds, or I should never have managed it with my volatile and impatient temperament, although I must admit that I made some bloomers along the way!

Much of a working gundog's training has to be instilled by the association of ideas. Such duties as hunting, use of nose and tender retrieving are, hopefully, hereditary and naturally 'stamped in'. What the trainer has to do is 'stamp out', or at least inhibit the development of, other natural tendencies such as chasing, taking in too much ground and the dog generally pleasing himself. General discipline, steadiness etc are taught, or stamped in, by the handler artificially using such aids as lead, voice and whistle, showing the pupil what to do by associating certain verbal and/or whistle/signal commands with the required actions. In other words, our aim is to channel a dog's instincts to work for us and not for himself by a course of graduated exercises over a long period, given in such a way that they appear almost as an enjoyable game to the dog which does not realise that he is being educated. You could almost use the term 'guiding' rather than 'training', because the emphasis is upon showing him how to do right before he gets the opportunity to do wrong, much in the same way as we try to bring up a child in the way it should go.

If you are to keep on the same wavelength as your pupil, retaining his trust and respect (known in the business as 'being at one with the dog'), so that he really wants to please you, *don't hurry the educational process*, especially the initial training course, in order to get him into the shooting field as quickly as possible. This is what so many fools do, and is the main reason why we see all those diabolical dogs out at shoots running-in, chasing every head of game that gets up, pinching game being carried by other dogs, flushing birds out of range etc. You've all seen them! This only leads to serious disagreement between handler and dog, loss of temper by the former and punishment of the latter, the reason for which he does not comprehend, the sum result being that the bond of confidence is seriously weakened if not completely broken. From then on the slope is likely to be steeply downwards and difficult, if not impossible, to reclimb.

Punishment

Correction can only be successfully effected if the dog knows the whys and wherefores of it which means catching him in the act of committing the crime. It is completely pointless to administer any rebuke afterwards, especially upon his return to you, and my heart sinks when I hear people say, 'he knew he had done wrong'. Dogs' minds just do not work like ours, it is up to us to make our minds work like theirs.

Let me quote the classic example of ill-conceived punishment which not only fails to produce the desired effect but completely defeats its own object and causes the dog to distrust and fear the handler. I refer to the case of a dog which roams away from home – a habit to which males in particular are very prone – but upon his return, tired, hungry and happy, all he receives in the way of greeting is a good 'going over' for being so naughty, given in the belief that the reason for it will be understood and heeded in future. Unfortunately the dog, by association of ideas, connects the punishment with his last act which was coming home. Consequently, the next time he goes off doing his own thing he will probably stop away even longer and be very reluctant to return home, fearing the hostile reception he received on the last occasion.

Another tragic mistake, commonly made by novice handlers, is to punish a dog for running-in to retrieve without orders when he returns carrying the bird. The poor dog hasn't got a clue that his crime was running-in, but associates the chastisement with his last action, which was retrieving to hand. Net result: the pupil loses confidence in, and becomes in fear of, the handler so that he refuses to deliver to hand in future, either making wary circles at a distance, or drops and refuses to bring on the retrieve, and some even become hard mouthed by gripping the bird too tightly in dread. Some refuse to retrieve at all.

In essence, the necessity for punishment is an admission of failure on the part of the handler because it is perfectly possible to educate a dog from start to finish without ever having to lay violent hands upon him. If you acquire a puppy of good working background at the optimum age of seven to eight weeks, and you bring him up 'according to the book' until old enough to commence a *thorough* training course of graduated lessons (usually when he is between six and nine months of age), he need never require more than a mild rebuke or a sharp slap *administered at the critical moment*.

It is essential to obtain and retain the trust and respect of the canine pupil, without which all efforts at training will be wasted. Gundog training can and should be great fun both for trainer and dog. It is much easier than many people believe but only if the trainer is prepared to be patient, study the subject beforehand and at all times try to see things from the dog's angle and endeavour to keep that one vital jump ahead and, above all, not be in too much of a damned hurry!

Choosing a Puppy

Anyone contemplating training a gundog is best advised to acquire a puppy as soon as he has been completely weaned, usually at around seven to eight weeks of age. Older puppies, especially those which have been living with the rest of the litter, are less adapatable to new surroundings and, to

Confident labrador pups, ready for new homes

a certain extent, will have already become set in their ways and have been influenced by the 'pecking order' which is established where several dogs are kept together. The younger the puppy the more quickly he will accept the handler as 'top dog' when removed from the pack influence, regard him as lord and master and generally prove trainable and receptive to his requirements. This gets management and education off to a flying start and lays the foundation of that vital bond of confidence and mutual respect between master (or mistress) and dog, without which attempts at training are a complete waste of time.

Of paramount importance is to ensure that you obtain the 'right tool for the job', in other words a puppy of *genuine working background and breeding*. Unfortunately today all the gundog breeds have become split into two camps, the show strains and the working strains. Quite honestly, trying to train a show-bred dog for the gun is equivalent to bashing your head against a brick wall! Of course there are the occasional exceptions but so few as to be negligible. So much so that all the reputable professional public trainers of my acquaintance refuse to take on any pupil whose pedigree indicates a preponderance of show breeding.

It is generally recommended that prospective working-gundog owners seek their puppies from parents with a field-trial winning background because this, to a very large extent, ensures that they have been bred for the job and have all the natural instincts and a high degree of trainability. I go along with this, but at the same time hasten to point out that there are scores of very solid and reliable dogs in private hands – gamekeepers and shooting folk of the old school in particular – which have never been near a field trial yet for generations have been proving their worth, week in and week out under field conditions, and a puppy with this sort of background should not be sneezed at.

If at all possible watch the parents – *particularly the dam* – at work when you go along to choose a puppy from a litter. Even during the close season you should be able to see her retrieving a dummy, note how well she responds to her handler's orders, her style of questing and courage in cover plus, of course, her general temperament. If you like what you see then you will probably be pretty safe in taking on one of her pups. Picking out an individual from the litter is always a risky business, but there are certain guidelines which help. Note particularly the puppy which is confident and comes up to you happily, does not flinch when you make a sudden movement or clap your hands loudly and, when you pay some attention to him, really looks at you with an intelligent expression. See the pups both in confined quarters and running about outside, both with and without their dam, and note their reactions.

Most well-bred pups of the retrieving breeds will have a natural instinct for the job so if you are picking a retriever, spaniel or one of the HPR (hunt, point, retrieve) breeds, ask the breeder to demonstrate the pups' ability with a small dummy or knotted handkerchief. As early as seven weeks they should pick up and carry, and even if they do run off in the opposite direction with their retrieve it proves a point.

I usually suggest to a novice owner seeking a puppy that he enlists the advice of a knowledgeable friend to help him arrive at a decision, because there are so many points to be considered. Not only the general condition and health of the puppy, which should be free from physical abnormalities which the inexperienced eye might not detect, but also the questions of pedigree, registration with the Kennel Club etc. If dealing with an established breeder

Choosing a puppy from a large litter is not easy

with a reputation to maintain most of these things can be taken for granted, and he will lean over backwards to help you in every way. However, if you go to a private (and possibly himself a novice) breeder, extreme caution is advisable. After all, puppies are not cheap (or, if they are, they are probably nasty!) and you are seeking a shooting companion which will hopefully last you for upwards of ten years, costing you quite a bit in upkeep along the way, so you want to start off with the right material.

Whether to have a dog or a bitch is a matter of personal preference, but if you are undecided consider these points. There is, in my opinion, a lot of truth in the old saying: 'A bitch is a nuisance twice a year [ie when she is in season] but a dog is a nuisance all the year round!' Generally speaking, bitches are easier to train and handle (and can usually be started younger than dogs), have less tendency to roam off and are less liable to be aggressive towards other dogs or humans. Of course there are many exceptions, and either sex can be neutered if really deemed necessary for obvious reasons, but I am not in favour of this. Firstly because it tends to cause the animal to put on excessive weight and alters his/her shape unless diet is very strictly rationed, and secondly because I have known so many owners regret having had the operation done (especially on bitches) because they would like to have been able to breed from their dogs which have turned out so well as workers and companions.

Once you have made your choice, for heaven's sake don't just pay up, shove the puppy into the car and dash back home in triumph. Spend some time with the breeder, pick his brains, and *write down his suggestions* about feeding and general management over the next few days or weeks because you must try to make the change-over as easy as possible for the pup, who will find it a traumatic experience for several days, missing mother and the rest of its family. Make a point of obtaining the paperwork, that is pedigree, Kennel Club documents and a veterinary certificate of any vaccinations given.

The puppy should already have been wormed once or twice. Note the date of the last dosing so that you can keep up this important routine at appropriate intervals. Your local veterinary surgeon will advise you on this and also supply necessary drugs. He will also put you into the picture about the vitally essential vaccinations which should be given against the many serious canine diseases: distemper, hepatitis, leptospirosis and the deadly canine parvo virus. Contact your vet immediately you have decided upon your pup, tell him the date of birth and start the course of injections as soon as he is prepared to give the first one. Be sure to advise him of any previous treatment.

For the first few weeks of life pups have a degree of immunity to diseases, gained from their dam's milk, but even so it is very dangerous to allow a pup to come into contact with other dogs, or exercise where other dogs have been, until the immunisation course has had time to take effect. This is generally about ten to fourteen days after the last injection. *You ignore these above warnings at your peril.* Like us, animals are more prone to disease when suffering from stress and a puppy recently removed from his family circle and being subjected to new and strange experiences (and people!) is bound to be stressed, even if it is not apparent.

The Formative Period

The time from weaning up to about the age of six months is the most formative period of a dog's life, during which the conscientious owner can lay the foundations of a successful future as a companion worker. On the other hand, the unthinking, impatient and possibly quick-tempered handler can – and not infrequently does – ruin his chances for all time, sometimes within days of taking him over. This is why it is so important for the novice owner to read up on the subject, pick the brains of more experienced owners and trainers, and get his priorities right before acquiring a dog. He can then start off on the right foot by making and keeping the dog happy and healthy, guiding him in such a way that he doesn't realise that he is being educated, so that he slots into both his domestic and sporting life quite naturally and without tears.

Forget any ideas you may have about starting *intensive* basic training (which is dealt with elsewhere in this book) until the puppy is between six and eight months of age, but concentrate upon the playschool and kindergarten stuff, so that he learns right from wrong and the general niceties of life without being repressed. Along the way your puppy can be given early and gentle experience of his basic duties as a gundog – retrieving, questing, facing cover etc – and also be accustomed to travelling in the car, a most important detail frequently left too late.

The Homecoming

Introduce your puppy to his new home as tactfully as possible, by which I mean don't let the kids maul him about and regard him as a new toy. By all means let him have plenty of your company, because you have to assert yourself as top dog and become his centre of interest, but remember also that pups, like all youngsters, human or canine, need plenty of rest and sleep, so let yours please himself in this respect.

You should already have decided whether to house the pup in a kennel, keep him indoors or combine the two systems. There is a lot to be said for making a dog versatile in this respect, because you may often find it more convenient to be able to kennel him up, such as when you are having a party, builders in the house or when you go away on holiday. Furthermore, in my experience once a dog commences his intensive training course he is far better kept in a kennel except when out for education and exercise. This means that he emerges full of get up and go, is pleased to see you and far more happy to concentrate upon lessons than the animal which has been loping round the house and garden all day and likely to be bored and lethargic.

The question of outside kennelling is dealt with elsewhere in this book, so I'll confine myself to suggestions for the 'indoors' dog. Some sort of bed must be provided, and I recommend a wooden box or plastic basket. Avoid the traditional (and still, for some obscure reason, popular) woven basket, which can be chewed up and both pups and adults are prone to use their teeth on it, especially if confined for long periods. Maybe I'm old fashioned, but I still prefer wood for my dogs to sleep upon, but the chewable edges and projections must be protected with metal. Plastic beds are subject to condensation, and a determined dog can still make inroads upon them when the mood takes him!

Bedding is a sore point with me! I believe it does more for the comfort and peace of mind of the owner than it does for the dog, and for nearly fifty years my dogs have slept healthily and happily on bare boards once past the puppyhood stage. Straw and hay not only encourage skin parasites but also get scattered and the dog ends up on the base of the bed anyway. Shredded paper, sheets of newspaper, an old carpet, or wood wool stuffed into strong sacking can be utilised if you *must* provide something, but it should be changed regularly and, obviously, can still be chewed and scattered. The modern so-called 'bean bags' (polystyrene pellets in reality) are certainly warm and comfortable, and liked by most dogs, but if the zip comes undone or the occupant chews or scratches the cover and makes a hole you'll have a lifetime's job clearing up!

House Training

There are also likely to be other clearing-up jobs around the house during the first few days for which you must be prepared until you have trained your puppy to be house-clean! No short answer to this, because pups vary greatly in their aptitude and a lot will depend upon what you are feeding and how often, how frequently he is let outside to 'do his duties' and whether he is of a nervous disposition.

Forget what you may have heard or read about rebuking by rubbing the pup's nose into his excrement and smacking him. It is quite useless and completely self-defeating, and makes a sensitive pup even more nervous. The best plan is to take him outside as frequently as possible, and *always directly after meals and last thing at night*. Don't feed after about 6 pm and put the pup outside really early in the morning. Be patient and make sure he 'obliges', and take him to the same spot in the garden each time until a pattern of cleanliness has become established. Dogs are by nature clean animals and dislike fouling their immediate environment once past the young puppyhood stage given the opportunity to empty themselves elsewhere. However adult males do have the embarrassing natural habit of marking their territory by cocking their legs in all sorts of strange places!

Feeding

As previously suggested you should follow the advice of the breeder and stick to the same diet that the pup has been accustomed to, at any rate for the first week or two. If you decide to change the type of food, do so very gradually in order not to upset his tummy.

For many years now my entire kennels have been fed on the 'complete diet pelleted system', used dry but with drinking water always available, with great success. This is used from puppyhood onwards and is not only very acceptable to the dogs but nourishing, extremely convenient and economical. Manufactured by Messrs Skinners, of Stradbroke, Eye, Suffolk, who offer a wide range of pelleted and meal foods as well as an excellent powdered milk for lactating bitches and pups, I can thoroughly recommend it. I am no lover of canned petfoods for many reasons.

From seven to twelve weeks of age I suggest pups are fed the puppy pellets morning and evening, with the milk drink only at midday. The milk is then discontinued, and the larger, adult type, pellets gradually substituted in place of the puppy pellets. However, you have to play this by ear according to how the pup is thriving, so the timing of the change-over is flexible. These all-in foods have a very impressive analysis and contain all the proteins, carbohydrates, minerals and vitamins etc essential to canine health, and they ensure that the dog passes firm and formed stools. An additional bonus is that they are extremely digestible and recommended by many vets for dogs which suffer from a condition known as endocrine pancreatic insufficiency, which is unfortunately becoming increasingly common.

'Playschool' Education

As soon as a puppy has settled down and accepted his new environment and handlers he can start learning the basics of his future duties without realising it, just like a three-year-old child attending playschool. This will enable him to slot comfortably into the intensive training course between six and nine months of age, and make life a lot easier for both dog and handler.

Gradually accustom your puppy to wearing a collar, which he will resent at first but soon accept, and then to walking on the lead. Don't drag and force him, rather use gentle persuasion. If you are tactful and patient, preferably when you have him outside in the garden for exercise and emptying, there should be no problems. Later on, when he is bigger and stronger, I suggest the use of a cord choke-type lead. Chain chokers I detest, and only ever used them on mature and recalcitrant dogs which could not be mastered by any other means. Incidentally, dogs which are being trained or worked in cover where there is any possibility of them becoming snagged up should never be wearing collars. Some terrible – even fatal – accidents have been caused when this obvious precaution has been neglected.

General exercise is most important, but *never allow a puppy to become tired out and exhausted*. I refer to free-running exercise, essential for both health and happiness. Indeed, it is a fact known to experienced handlers that dogs think far more of the person who gives them exercise than they do of the one who feeds them, contrary to popular belief. Sedentary toddles round the block on the end of a lead may suffice during the very early days, but as the pup

A useful type of webbing slip-choke lead

grows he must be able to gallop about unfettered to develop muscle and stamina and as an aid to digestion. The amount of exercise to give is largely a matter of commonsense, and you must graduate it according to the reactions, condition and age of your puppy. Little and often is a good maxim, which should also apply to lessons throughout the entire educational curriculum.

All working gundogs, sooner or later, have to deal with cover of some sort, and valuable groundwork can be laid during exercise periods. I am not suggesting that an eight-week-old puppy should be asked to dive into a formidable bramble patch, but by giving him short walks in tall grass and subsequently other suitable cover of gradually increasing density, according to reaction and progress, he will come to regard cover as a natural and enjoyable element. Obviously you must be guided by the age and size of your puppy, again a matter for commonsense, and, above all, keep him happy and enjoying what he is doing. Don't forget that a gundog needs to have courage and enthusiasm if he is to do his job properly, and you can ruin both at an early age if you're not very careful. Always take the weather conditions into consideration, especially avoiding extremes of temperature.

Retrieving, Dummies, Commands and Whistles

During these exercise jaunts a moderate amount of retrieving practice can be given to the appropriate breeds. The operative word is *moderate*, because a puppy will quickly sicken if he is continually being asked to fetch, and may end up by refusing to lift and carry, or start running off with the dummy and burying it! *Retrieving should be a privilege and not a chore*, and once a puppy has proved himself keen on the job, picks up and delivers happily, practice should be strictly limited and diversified by the dummy being hidden instead of thrown in full view.

The very young puppy must obviously have a small dummy, which can be anything from a rolled up and knotted handkerchief, a child's sock stuffed with rags, an old leather glove or anything soft to the custom-made canvas puppy dummy. As he gets older and bigger so the size and weight of the dummies can be increased, and the more variation offered the better. A suitably sized ball can also be used occasionally, and is convenient to carry in the pocket.

To start with the dummy should be thrown a short distance in full view of the pupil who will, hopefully, run in, pick up and return to hand in triumph. Later on he will have to learn to await orders before retrieving, but at this stage we are trying to establish enthusiasm, confidence, prompt return and willing delivery. If all goes well, *gradually* extend the distance the dummy is thrown, and also start lofting it so that it is hidden in cover (tall

grass for instance) so that your pupil has to start using his nose and really search for it. But all this must be done over a long period as the puppy grows and progresses and, again I emphasise, make haste slowly and don't try to do too much at a time.

Your puppy should already have been taught his name, so immediately his head goes down to pick up the dummy encourage him by calling, and if he doesn't come immediately, starts playing with it or runs off in the opposite direction, walk quickly away – or even run! This usually has the desired result. Take the dummy from him gently, and don't, whatever you do, engage in a tug of war. Praise and pat him, and then leave well alone until the next day.

At this stage you should also introduce the appropriate command for retrieving such as 'fetch' (and be sure you stick to it) as the puppy dashes out to pick up, and also start to use the recall whistle, either mouth made or artificial. Whistle commands will be useful throughout the entire training course, as will be explained elsewhere. Dogs respond to them well once taught and they are less disturbing to game than the human voice. I favour a series of short 'pips' for recall whistle, which should be blown immediately after calling the pup's name so that, ultimately, the vocal call can be discontinued and the whistle alone used. In due course the whistle should also be used as a 'stop-sit' command, for which I suggest a single sharp blast, and the pup accustomed to it in a similar manner to the above.

Discipline

Ultimately our young pupil has got to learn to sit immediately upon command, wherever he may be in relation to the handler, because this is what I term the 'king-pin of training'. However, it is a mistake to start teaching it too early. *Intensive* sit-stay lessons inhibit the pup and make him 'sticky' and may cause confusion in his mind. The *basic* idea can be instilled at feeding time quite easily. All you have to do is stand and hold the feedbowl whilst pup is dancing round your feet in glorious anticipation. Before long I bet you'll see him sit down and gaze at you expectantly, at which moment utter the 'sit' command, keep him waiting a few seconds and then put his grub down.

This practice will also make the pup interested in your hand movements, which will be valuable later on when more serious training commences and hand signals become important. Incidentally, similar hand-watching, and probably also automatic sitting, will be fostered during retrieving practice by tantalising him by fondling the dummy for a few seconds just before you throw it out, when, again, the operative word to sit can be given. All gradually and painlessly building up to the more serious work ahead.

I should have mentioned before that useful word 'no', uttered in stern tones, to stop wrongdoing, because it really can work wonders and I wouldn't be without it! Sometimes it may have to be accompanied by repressive action

A well constructed (and obviously comfortable!) dog travelling box

on your part, but is usually quickly learned and subsequently heeded. Dogs are very responsive to the tone of your voice and, indeed, many of the more sensitive ones can be controlled by this alone. Try to give the usual commands quietly but firmly, and save the gruff, grumbling and loud shouts for emergencies!

Do, please, be consistent throughout training, both with commands and actions. For instance, it may be all very well to allow a tiny puppy to jump up at you or sit on your lap, but you'll be furious when a 50lb muddy monster does likewise later on, so start off as you mean to go on. Decide upon the commands you are going to use, and stick to them always, unless you want a confused dog on your hands.

Humanising, Travel and Noises

See as much of your pup as you can, and take him out to encounter people and things, but do all this gradually and never force him into situations which appear to frighten him. Don't encourage other people to fuss him or feed him tit-bits, as so many misguided folk tend to do, especially in pubs. Keep him under control in public places and prevent him from making a nuisance of himself. I strongly disapprove of owners who tow their dogs, puppy or adult, round country fairs and the like, which smacks of exhibitionism and, I am convinced, is not enjoyed by the dogs and even less so by members of the public who trip over their leads!

Experience of travelling in the car should be given both early and gradually. Many dogs suffer from travel sickness and far too many owners give up the battle against constant drooling or vomiting instead of persevering. Short journeys to start with, essentially on an empty stomach (the puppy I mean) which should have an enjoyable conclusion such as a good spell of free-running exercise. Some dogs which take a dislike to the car can be cured by being fed therein whilst it is standing in the drive or the garage, which associates the vehicle with something pleasant. Sickness can also be caused by the build-up of static electricity, as with human sufferers, and fitting the car with an earthing chain or strap will obviate this. The use of travel sickness pills should be avoided unless all else fails, because they make the dog a bit dopey for quite a time and, anyway, are only an admission of defeat. I can thoroughly recommend the use of car travelling boxes if properly constructed, and most dogs soon accept them as a 'home from home'. They also save on wear and tear on the car's upholstery and, if a mess is accidentally made, it is confined to the box and easily cleaned up.

Noise shyness can almost always be prevented by good and tactful management. The time to accustom your pup to noises of increasing loudness is when you feed him. Many breeders make a practice of banging the kennel wall or the feedbowl, giving loud handclaps etc as a 'grub's up' signal to the litter as soon as they start taking solid food, which really does work wonders. The private owner of a single pup can extend upon this with ingenuity, leading up to the time when the sound of the shotgun can be introduced, fired at a distance by an assistant at the moment the food bowl is placed before the puppy. But, whatever else you do, for heaven's sake don't make the common and extremely dangerous mistake of carting your young puppy round to clay pigeon shoots in the belief that this is the answer to the noise question. Believe me it is not and is much more likely to completely defeat the object.

It only remains for me to wish you good luck with your gundog puppy and express the hope that I have written enough to put you on the right lines for the further education of your future shooting companions. I will leave you with one final thought and suggestion: if things go wrong in training don't press on regardless, but stop, think and seek expert advice if necessary. It's probably your fault, anyway!

Simon

JOHN HUMPHREYS

I knew nor cared not whence he came, he seemed to have been there always, but for a very first family dog such things did not matter. What were affairs of pedigree or origin to a child of six? What could such a one know of breeding, of training for the gun, of obedience – in himself, let alone in a dog?

His name was Simon, a flop-eared Welsh springer spaniel, patient in a way which belies the breed's reputation, for with hindsight we children were lucky to escape with no more than the odd nip for all our unthinking unkindnesses. You see, we were not a shooting household save that father, a country parson by profession, would make the odd sally into the garden when the pigeons had tried even his Christian tolerance too far and cropped his sprouting cauliflowers down to bare stalks. He would steal down the garden in the shadow of the shrubbery and loose a blast from his old single barrel. The damage resulting from this volley was far greater than any number of pigeons would have committed, but his satisfaction at a rogue brought to book made him overlook the line of shattered stalks which appeared as though a scythe had been through them, showing where his deadly shot had raked.

One sensed that after a while he was not as happy at his success as he pretended, for deep down he did not care to kill things and in the end he decided that the birds had as much right to eat as he did and the pigeons took full advantage, in spite of which his brassicas still seemed to do as well as those of anybody else.

Simon was a pet, there on the hearthrug, the proper place for traditional dogs, poddling about the rambling lawns and shrubbery, lying asleep in the sun or going about his business and visiting his friends along the dusty high street. Those were not the days of speeding traffic: a horse and cart was the common mode of conveyance, that and the trusty fenland bicycle or more rarely the sight of the squire's early Wolseley, clattering and smoking but rarely exceeding the driver's self-imposed speed limit of 25mph, was the sum of what you might encounter in the village in those dusty, and everlastingly sunny, days.

25

Those were the times when we knew the local dogs as well as the people, smiled and greeted them when we met them, farmer's stackyard curs, terriers yapping in the yard of the local ratter, house dogs and the rare, ill-trained gundog. We knew them all and dear old Simon took his place in this local subculture and as 'parson's dog' was generally liked and respected.

As my age reached the coveted goal of double figures, I took to the gunning, an almost universal pastime in my village. There was no TV at which to gawp and waste God-given hours, no bingo, no public transport to speak of, very little of anything in fact. You made your own pleasures. The air rifle had come, been mastered and was already losing its appeal. I wanted greater fire power for I was adept at creeping like a snake down a summer hedgerow and stalking the powdery, feathered woodpigeon which sat cooing in the long evenings, all innocence on top of the stunted Scots pine. Sparrows fell in droves to my deadly .177 slugs, I could shoot a match head and make it light and even hit a penny held rather nervously between the thumb and forefinger of my childhood partner in crime.

My path of escape and enlightenment lay through the sexton, a gnarled man of indeterminate age, a waistcoat and silver watch chain, a flat hat and thin as a pike. In the shed which housed his digging tools he kept a rusty twelve bore, only one barrel of which would fire, the other having the hammer spring broken and a sizeable hole halfway up the barrel. He would be digging away when, with a clatter of wings, a pigeon settled in one of the vicarage elms. In an instant that old man was transformed into a stealing panther, a snake in the grass as, using the only available cover, he crept from 'RIP' to 'Dearly Beloved Husband . . .' When he had reached a suitable place a knobbly thumb would draw back the hammer, careful aim would be taken, there would be a massive explosion and puff of smoke and, without even opening its wings, the bird would tumble down into the nettles and keks below whence the old chap would rush to retrieve it.

That was the idea all right! I watched him from my bedroom window often rushing out from breakfast as the family rose in collective alarm at the unexpected sound of his single, deadly shot echoing through the garden and into the open window. I wanted to see what he had shot this time, for he rarely missed. In the mating season he quite often got two birds at once, giving a new meaning to interruptus.

Elsewhere I have recounted how the grudging loan of this weapon came to me. The air rifle had its limitations: it was possible to hit a pigeon fair and square amidships and still it was not mortally wounded and, with a squirt of white feathers, it would fly off strongly to be lost forever. At last those frustrations were behind me and using my stalking skills and diminutive size, I could creep along with this rattle trap of a gun and shoot pigeons for the sexton and, of course, everything I shot became his.

Something was wrong, and I felt sure I had heard somewhere that such a gun was intended to shoot quarry on the move and not sitting passively in a tree or, in the case of rabbits, nibbling the grass quite unaware of the awful danger which threatened. I asked my mentor about this and, rolling himself the slenderest of cigarettes, he thought for a moment and gave the considered opinion that, 'Guns is for gintlemen and fules and I ain't none o' them.' That was the last word surely; the oracle had spoken. But, small though I was I proved him wrong. Walking down the garden one day, past the dilapidated greenhouse, along the place where, in headier days a carefully mown tennis court lay, a pigeon came blundering out of the elders 10yd in front of me. In a rash moment, for cartridges were costly enough not to be squandered in such recklessness, the gun found the shoulder and effortlessly a shot was fired, the bird crumpled and fell. The recoil which I had come to dread, was strangely absent and my heart was full to overflowing with wild elation which even now I feel when I recall that moment.

There was more to come, for, as the bird crashed and fell with such exhilarating finality, there dashed a brown blur from behind me and, quite unexpectedly, Simon entered the fray, rushed in to the fall, picked the pigeon up as lightly as thistledown and brought it to me, laying it gently at my feet. Not only my first flying shot, but my first retrieve with a proper gundog; not bad for one moment of madness. After that, Simon dogged my footsteps for, although never trained for the gun, he had the ancient breeding in him and nettles which for me in my shorts were agony were to him a pleasure if one of my pigeons lay hidden in their fastness. First hand, and in the most positive way, I learned the pleasure and also the usefulness of a shooting dog.

Sadly, the old chap was already an aged pensioner when first he showed me what he could do. To a child a dog will live forever just as nothing in his world will ever change, but it was not to be. I had not realised that he was growing old and that twilight was upon him, and one day when he did not come to my morning whistle my mother broke the sad news. There was not, as they say, a dry eye in the house for we all deeply mourned his loss. It was to be some years before we had another dog, after which I was never again to be without one, but that was indeed a poignant moment.

Simon was buried under the apple tree and often I thought of him, although sterner affairs such as going away to school and leaving the village for long periods broke the chains, sweet chains though they were, and shooting was not to return to my head for another five years.

Simon I will always remember, the first dog we owned, the first dog I saw retrieve and most of all, one which showed me the pleasures of shooting in canine company. For that if for nothing else I have much to thank the old boy, for they were two lessons I was never to forget.

Basic Training

ROY JORDAN

Roy Jordan worked as an industrial chemist for forty-two years at the research centre of the Dunlop Company. He served for six years in the Royal Navy during the war on destroyers where he was twice wounded and mentioned in dispatches. He has trained dogs for over thirty years and has competed in obedience and tracking trials as well as working tests and field trials. He has been a dog trainer for ten years with the German Shorthaired Pointer Club, ten years with the United Retriever Club and seventeen years with the Midland Gundog Society. He is BASC Gundog Advisor and is currently running gundog courses for the BASC.

If you have purchased a young puppy it is most important that he be allowed to accustom himself to the sights and sounds of everyday life and here I must mention the fallacy that it is essential for a gundog to live in a kennel. I certainly do not believe that this is true, as one frequently finds that a dog living in the house achieves a better understanding with his owner. However, it is certainly a good idea to provide a kennel so that the dog may be put out of the way when desired. One important fact to note is that the dog should never be allowed to roam free about the countryside or roads on his own.

To commence puppy training at about ten weeks, first place a plain leather collar around the puppy's neck for a short period each day. Slip chains are not recommended at this stage. You will find at first that the puppy will spend his time endeavouring to scratch the collar off but after a few days will completely ignore it. Following this, attach a light lead to the puppy's collar and encourage him to go for a short walk with you. During this period the lesson should not exceed five minutes at any time, as this is the first attempt for you to obtain co-operation and confidence from your puppy; great patience must be shown.

One of the first jobs is to construct suitable accommodation

You will find that the puppy frequently just wants to sit down. When this happens he should not be tugged but gently encouraged in a happy voice. As your puppy grows, you will find that he is constantly carrying around a series of objects. This should be encouraged, however revolting the objects may be. Encourage him at this stage to bring the article he is carrying to you. Attempt to take the article from him but do not engage in a tug of war with your puppy. Choose a suitable command such as 'give' and place your hand underneath the jaw, thumb and forefinger either side of the puppy's jaw. Very gently exert pressure as far back as possible between the two jaws, the puppy's mouth will open and the object may be gently removed. At the same time the puppy should be praised. The puppy should never be shouted at whatever he may be carrying even when it is your best shoe or favourite glove. Care must be taken to see that these objects are placed out of reach at all times.

General Training

When the puppy is about six months old general training may start although if the puppy is bold this may start a little earlier. Should you have a timid puppy it must be left until later. Basic obedience training is the first

When you stop, the dog should sit

essential for any puppy, and commands should be given first by voice. Use short words and say them firmly and distinctly so that he is not confused. Since the puppy does not understand words it does not matter what word you choose; you can even invent your own, but once the puppy has learned the meaning of whatever word you choose, stick to this word and do not use alternative commands or speak in sentences; this will only confuse. In general do not repeat commands once he knows their meaning. If he does not obey it is likely to be because he did not hear you.

First the puppy must be taught to sit on command. This is done by having him on the collar with the lead on your left-hand side. Take the lead in your right hand and place your left hand on the puppy's hindquarters. Using the command 'sit' pull the puppy's head up with the lead and with your left hand push his hindquarters down to the ground. When the puppy is in the sitting position praise him and allow him to get up again. This must be repeated several times at intervals and must be practised until the dog associates the command with the action of sitting.

The next stage when the puppy has learned to sit, is the command 'stay'. To do this have him in the sitting position. Raise your right arm and step slowly across in front of the puppy to face him and use the command 'stay'. Keep your right arm raised still holding the lead which should be kept fairly taut. If the puppy attempts to move pull the lead up sharply and repeat the command 'stay'. Never use the puppy's name in giving the command 'stay', as this will only induce him to move. When you are sure the puppy will remain sitting whilst you are standing immediately in front of him, keep your right hand raised, slowly lower the lead to the ground and retreat one pace. Keep the puppy in this position for a few seconds and slowly return

Hand signals should be positive

'Heel'

to his side. Should he attempt to rise, repeat the command 'sit' followed by the command 'stay'. This exercise should be practised several times a day. When you are quite certain the puppy is steady, gradually lengthen the distance you leave him and also the length of time. At this stage always return to the puppy rather than calling him to you, which may encourage him to leave the 'stay' position before you wish him to.

Teaching the puppy to walk to heel is another very important lesson. Have him on the lead on your left-hand side. Step off smartly calling his name followed by the command 'heel'. Walk at a good pace and if the puppy pulls to the side or the front jerk his lead smartly back repeating the command 'heel'. This exercise should be practised for about ten minutes each day. As the puppy learns to walk to heel, the lead can be slackened more and more until eventually you can drop the lead completely and allow it to trail.

At this stage, when you have to stop, the puppy should be made to sit at your side. It is important that your puppy should be made to come right up to you when he is called. This will ensure a good delivery later on. Should he not come straight in when called, it is best to teach the recall as an exercise. This should be done by placing the dog on a light check cord about 10yd long, commanding him to 'stay' and backing slowly away, paying out the cord as you go. Keep the puppy sitting steady for approximately half a minute, then call his name and give the command 'heel'. If he does not respond at once, jerk firmly on the cord and pull it in. Even if he is originally being disobedient, praise your pupil when he eventually reaches you.

The Whistle

When you have the puppy obeying verbal commands, the whistle should be introduced, as this is a much quieter method of controlling your dog and is less disturbing when there is game about. There are two main whistle commands: the stop and the come-in. The 'stop' command is a long drawn out whistle and the 'come-in' command is a series of short whistles. First, to teach him to stop to the whistle, have him walking to heel and each time you stop, blow a long blast on the whistle and make him sit. To teach him to come into the whistle, do the 'stay' exercise and then call him in with short blasts on the whistle instead of using your voice. When he has got these two whistle commands firmly in his mind, make him sit and stay then call him in to you with several short blasts on the whistle. When he is about halfway towards you, raise your right hand and blow a long blast on the whistle to make him sit where he is. It will take several lessons before he can perfect this exercise.

You are now ready to take your puppy and introduce him to the smells of the countryside. The puppy should never be allowed to run wild in the

'His name was Simon, a flop-eared Welsh springer spaniel . . .'

Black labrador clears a fence in fine style

countryside or you cannot possibly expect him to be obedient later on. He should be taken into well-wooded country where there is plenty of rough cover. He should be encouraged to hunt in all the cover but should not, however, be allowed to roam too far. He should not be loose for too long at a time. He should be allowed a few minutes running loose and hunting and then should be called back to heel again. In this way he will become used to being always under control when out in the countryside. As the puppy grows older and more accustomed to the smells of game, he will quickly get out of hand if not kept strictly under control.

Introduction to Gunfire

Introduction to gunfire should take place at this stage, but must be handled very carefully. The puppy should previously have been accustomed to everyday sounds such as banging doors, dropping of food dishes, bursting of paper bags and other noises. Should he show any signs of nervousness, any introduction to noise should be taken more slowly. Some puppies are born with a certain degree of sound shyness, but in most cases this can be overcome if treated carefully. A puppy which is genuinely sound shy becomes worse as more noise is introduced and cannot be accustomed to any noise. This stems from a deep-rooted fear and the sound-shy puppy should be discarded as far

Much of your puppy's early life should be spent in play

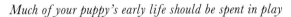

as gundog work is concerned. When you are assured that the puppy shows no signs of nervousness at any bangs or sudden noise, enlist the help of a friend with a gun. Find a suitable spot where the puppy an be approximately 100yd away from where the gun is fired. If the puppy is unperturbed by the shot, take him a little closer but always watch him for any reaction to the shot. It is often a good plan to make a fuss of the puppy while he is getting used to the sound of gunfire. Remember, little and often is always better than one long lesson. It is of the utmost importance that the fundamental obedience work that he has just learned is consistently obeyed before the dog is taken onto the next stage of his training.

Dummy Training

It is now time to start dummy training. There are several methods of making dummies, ranging from stuffing material into an old sock, rolling up strips of canvas or the more elaborate types of rabbit or hareskin dummies. Usually the sock dummy stuffed with a soft material weighing about ½lb is the best type of dummy to start your puppy on. Later, the weight should be increased to at least 1lb.

Puppies vary considerably in their attitude towards retrieving. Some are

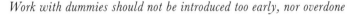

Work with dummies should not be introduced too early, nor overdone

For every five dummies thrown, the trainer should retrieve four himself

madly keen to fetch everything all the time, others at first show no interest in the exercise at all. The very eager puppy must be restrained carefully until the dummy has been thrown, whilst the reluctant puppy may be allowed to run in to encourage him to pick up the dummy. When your puppy is confidently picking-up and carrying his dummy you should teach him the correct retrieve exercise. Make him sit and stay beside you and if he is very eager he may, at first, need to be put on a lead. Again enlist the help of a friend. Your friend should stand about 20yd away and attract the puppy's attention. He should then throw the dummy into the air for it is easier for the puppy to mark it. Do not send the puppy straight away to fetch the dummy as this will eventually encourage him to run in. Make him wait several seconds then use a suitable command such as 'fetch' and send him out for the dummy. As soon as he has picked it up, whistle him back to you. Take the dummy very carefully and make a great fuss of him. If he is reluctant to bring the dummy right up to you or runs away with it, do not chase him as he may think it is a game. Walk away and he will soon learn that he should bring the dummy straight to you. Never ask the puppy to retrieve more than twice in one outing as this is an exercise which can very easily be overdone.

When he is retrieving confidently make the retrieves a little more diffi-cult. Take the dummy into the rough cover so that he really has to hunt for it. Gunfire should not be introduced with the retrieve until the puppy is completely steady, otherwise he may tend to run in to shot. When you are satisfied that he is really under control enlist the help of someone who can fire the gun for you, as at first you will need all your attention on the puppy. Eventually you will be able to fire the gun and control the puppy yourself.

Training to retrieve from water is another important exercise. For this, a slightly different dummy is required as, of course, it must float. An easy way to make a water dummy is to get an old washing-up liquid container and cover it with a familiar sock. This will float well and is easily and readily picked up by the puppy. Some dogs love water and will swim from the earliest days, but others need a great deal of encouragement at first. A fast-flowing river must be avoided when commencing water retrieving as the dummy will get carried far downstream and steep banks should also be avoided because if the puppy is a bit cautious this will certainly put him off and he will also find difficulty in getting out of the water and up the bank. Try and find a quiet river or a pond with a gentle slope into it. With a puppy who is bold in water he should straight away be taught the retrieve exercise in the same way as he was taught on land. If however the puppy is very doubtful about this new element, throw the dummy in only at the very edge where the puppy can paddle in and get it without having to swim first.

Directional Control

When you feel quite sure that the puppy has mastered the exercises which you have done so far, it is time to proceed with directional control. Take two similar dummies, sit your puppy in an open space and stand immediately in front of him as you did in the 'sit' and 'stay' exercises. Giving the command 'stay' to your puppy, throw one dummy to the left and one to the right, making sure that your puppy does not move. Take two paces back.

When first teaching this exercise it is best to send the puppy for the dummy which you threw first, that is if the right-hand dummy was thrown first raise your right arm above your head and indicate with a downward movement to the right that the puppy is to go for that particular dummy. At the same time give the command 'fetch'. When he has retrieved this dummy, again sit him in front of you in the same place. Raise your left hand and indicate to the dog that he is to fetch the left-hand dummy. Always give a clear downward sweep of the arm when doing this exercise and simultaneously give the command 'fetch'. It will be some time before the puppy understands these exercises and they must be practised carefully over a long period, but no single lesson should last for more than about ten minutes.

As the puppy becomes more sure of himself, step further back until you can direct him from a distance of about 30yd. When he is really confident in fetching the two dummies at your direction, it is time to introduce a third dummy which is thrown behind him. When he is sent for this dummy the command 'get back' should be given. There should be a forward movement with your right arm. Again gradually increase the distance from which you

Advanced dummy work: the dog must retrieve the one for which he is sent

direct the puppy. At any time during this training, if the puppy appears to become confused, always go back to a previous exercise that he has really understood so that he should finish the training lesson on a happy note.

Direction onto Hidden Dummies

The next stage in the control exercise is to direct your dog onto a hidden dummy from a distance. Hide the dummy and then place your puppy in a position so that you are able to stand a few yards in front of him and give him a left-hand signal when you are commanding him to fetch the dummy. Do not place the dummy more than 20yd away at first. Make sure the puppy always finds the dummy even if, in the end, you have to take him to where it lies. Repeat this exercise varying the direction in which you send the puppy, either back, left or right and increase the distance from where you give the directions. All this will take a great deal of time and patience but the puppy must not be hurried if he is to understand these directions completely.

Another variation on this control exercise is to send your puppy for a hidden dummy when he has already marked a dummy thrown in the opposite direction. As the temptation to run in after the one dummy is now becoming greater for the puppy, the handler must always be ready with a whistle to blow 'stop' immediately he sees the puppy going in the wrong direction and to make a clear hand signal to show the right direction. For the breeds which hunt, point and retrieve, this directional control is even more important, since the hand signals are used for directing the dog to where he should hunt for live game as well as for directing him to his retrieves.

Steadiness

Teaching the dog steadiness under the many and varying temptations which occur in the shooting field is perhaps the main difficulty in training. This aspect of work takes time, understanding and patience, but is of great importance because, although most gundogs will hunt and even retrieve quite naturally, unless they are controlled, the chances are that they will spoil more sport than they provide. Many people have discoverd that it is not simply the amount of game killed but the enjoyment achieved in retrieving it that counts on the shooting day.

Collars

Before you ask a dog to enter cover in search of a dummy or for any other reason, remember that it is most important to take off his collar. A working gundog, when he is expected to hunt in cover amongst thick brambles and hedges, should never have anything around his neck which might get tangled

If you have more than one dog, a pecking order will soon be established

up and cause him to choke. In the event of a metal collar touching an electric fence, there could be serious consequences.

Scent

Scent and scenting conditions are prime factors in gundog training and in order to give the dog full advantage of this, note must be taken of the wind direction when working him. The dog should always be allowed to work downwind of the object he is scenting. Control and directional exercises should also be practised when doing water work, as scent is something that human beings cannot understand. It frequently happens that a dog appears to miss something in water and this can only be because he had not been able to scent it properly, yet to an observer the object may seem a simple retrieve.

HPR Breeds

Basic training for the pointing breeds can be carried out as for retrievers, but the elements you now want to concentrate on are quartering and pointing which come naturally to most dogs and include pointing at anything and everything from gamebirds to songbirds in a hedge. All the time encourage the dog to stay and point no matter what it is. As soon as he goes on point approach the dog from the side and put him on his lead. Stay with the dog and keep him on point as long as he wants to while you encourage. Then drop the dog as you flush the quarry. No rules of training are infallible and the trainer should always have an open mind. Not all dogs will achieve the same standards, however well they are trained. There are always some that have a greater capacity for work and a far more deeply engraved instinct than others.

Punishment

It is useless to punish a dog unless he associates the punishment with what he has done wrong. For example, a dog which fails to come or runs away when called will only be encouraged to do the same if he is chastised when he does come in. To praise him for coming in may be difficult if he has annoyed you, but this is the only effective remedy. Hitting a dog is of little value as a punishment. The slapping noise made by the flat of the hand on the thigh can be effective if administered just as the crime is about to be committed or is being committed. Tone of voice too is most useful and the handler should cultivate distinctly different 'good boy' and 'bad boy' terms which will be readily recognised by the dog. For the determined wrongdoer who knows he is doing wrong, the best remedy is to grab the dog by the scruff of the neck on each side of the head and hold him facing towards you. Then give him a good shake at the same time telling him what you think of

him in your 'bad-boy' voice. Then make a show of putting him on the lead and make him walk to heel or sit for a while.

Travelling

Practically every working gundog these days has to be accustomed to travelling by car and this very often presents quite a problem, particularly if you have a dog which is prone to car sickness. It is a very good idea, particularly with young dogs, that they be allowed time in the car whilst it is stationary at home before being taken for a ride which, for the first time, should be of a very short duration. Should the car you possess be a saloon and not of the estate variety, there are some very good light travelling boxes on the market which many people prefer so that the car does not get spoiled by a wet and muddy dog at the end of a shooting day. These boxes are heartily recommended. A wash leather is very good for drying a dog or, of course, an ordinary towel and is a very small burden to add to your normal shooting equipment. Do not leave your dog in a parked car for long periods and never leave him inside if the windows are closed or if it is very hot. Teach the dog to wait before getting in or out of the vehicle. It is very dangerous if the dog leaps out as soon as the door of the vehicle is opened.

Exercise

Everyday exercise is the most important factor in the dog's life and it is cruel to keep a dog confined to a kennel except for shooting days because exercise not only keeps him fit but his mind alert and strengthens his bond with the handler. Normal exercise should consist of a good run with the dog allowed free both morning and evening with additional exercise if possible during midday. To allow a dog loose in a small garden or paddock is not sufficient, as he will not exercise himself under these conditions.

Bitches on Heat

If you have a bitch you must be prepared to take special precautions when she comes on heat. Make sure that the dogs cannot get at her and in order to dissuade the inevitable retinue of male admirers, try and exercise her as far away from home as possible. She should not be allowed to roam free at this time unless you are prepared to have puppies of doubtful parentage. If you live in a town and have to walk her from home, there are several preparations which will reduce her attractiveness to dogs. Owners of male dogs too will have to keep their dogs under very strict control when a bitch in the neighbourhood is in season. Even if he cannot actually reach her a roaming dog often sets up a passionate and annoying howling from the nearest vantage point. In addition, when there is a bitch in season a dog will quickly lose condition despite any extra food which you may give him at this time. A bitch on heat should not be taken shooting if there is even a remote chance of a male dog being out with the party.

Ajax

JOHN HUMPHREYS

What a name! I was into the Ancient Greeks at the time and there was a great warrior of that name who distinguished himself mightily before the gates of Troy. It was to my dismay that a few months after the christening, a sink cleaner appeared on the market bearing the same name. So it was as 'the Foaming Cleanser' my poor dog was nicknamed by wags in the village. In fact both names were entirely inappropriate, for he was by no means a mighty man of iron and slaughter but a gentle old thing, and any action less like 'foaming' it would be hard to imagine.

I was an unlovable teenager, dissatisfied with life, at odds with my parents and generally disgruntled, a feeling I guess that all of us have experienced during our mid-teens. Ajax was bought by my father, bless his heart, as a rift-healer, and he arrived in a cardboard box, with a scrap of sacking in the bottom. My poor father was no great judge of dogs and I suspect that Ajax was the only one left, he was the one that all previous purchasers had rejected. He was a pure-bred labrador with no paper credentials and he came from Chatteris way somewhere. His colour was the palest of yellow, almost white, and he had a thick coat, aquiline nose and gentle eye.

What I knew of dog training could be written with a felt-tipped pen on a pin-head; I thought they were all like the late lamented Simon and just picked it up as they went along. I was a great tramper of the wild Fens in those days, the sexton's gun having been mercifully replaced by a local 'farm gun', also a double-barrel hammer weapon from the same stable, but both hammers worked, there was no hole along the barrel and the gun was tight and sound. Like all of its pedigree it was deemed 'a good killer' and so it should have been, for all those old imported, rusty guns were all but innocent of choke. I should have learned at that time, but failed to, the truth of the old saying that 'all choke is the invention of the Devil'.

This is how it used to be. Up early, a snatched breakfast and straight down to the fen known as the America – not that surprising, really, for we also boasted an Africa and a Botany Bay, all names of former colonies, for the early fenland settlers

44

must have felt like missionaries as they established their colonies in those hazardous, marginal waterlands. I travelled on my father's old college Hercules which I had cunningly converted to take a gun. A leather strap hung from the handlebars and a deep wire hook padded with tape hung from the saddle stem. The hook took the stock of a gun below the trigger-guard and the strap held the barrels. In this way I could, and did, ride many a bumpy mile with never a mishap.

Ajax loped along, his nose hard by my back wheel, and at an easy pace we freewheeled down the hill, flattened out at the bottom where the houses ended and then we could contemplate the vast purple-brown and misty distance of the great fen with the golden apple of a sun fretted by a row of bankside willows. Partridges were calling from near and far, before and behind and from all sides.

A mile later we swung into a dilapidated farmyard. Chickens scratched and laid their eggs in the straw stacks; pigs grunted from their makeshift sty; broken machinery which was new when Turnip Townsend first donned gaiters stood like great dinosaur skeletons in rank nettles where they had been abandoned to the rust. The scent was an amalgam of chaff, old straw, peat, farm animals and dry potato haulms. What would I not give for a whiff of it now?

Blessings on the kind farmers who allowed me the freedom to shoot their small farms. The holdings ran together, all small fields, a stooked stubble like an Indian encampment giving way to 10 acres of browned-off potatoes which in turn became a square of shiny sugar-beet. Norfolk reed was common to them all, a straggly beard of it creeping out from each boundary dyke. Wild oats were a problem; fat hen, willow herb and loosetrife all flourished while the moths and butterflies flew in clouds. A pheasant was rare, but hares and mallard were common while as for partridges . . . Does memory delude me or did every field, especially the weedy potatoes hold at least three good covies? Do I lie when I claim that it was common for me to come home with ten brace of them to my own gun?

I hid the cycle in the lee of a tumbled straw stack, shouldered the feathery canvas bag which also contained my sandwich, limbered my rusty fowling piece and walked across the yard and into the first field. Accompanied only by Ajax, my method was simply to quarter the quiet acres back and forth until Ajax or I had covered every inch of it. His lack of training was regrettable but he had taught himself more or less what to do and in so doing, taught me. I did need to break into a trot now and then to keep up with him and we never could agree about the correct procedure for hares, but he was a dear gentle thing, and many a good deed and nifty retrieve more than made up for the times when I could have happily slaughtered him, all my own fault and not his.

We tried to walk upwind and there were techniques for working each crop. Potatoes we crossed from ridge to ridge, easier than walking along the rows and you had a better chance of stumbling into a covey. The farmer would complain if you kicked out too much of the crop to green in the fierce suns of late autumn. In sugar-beet we waded along the rows, quickly learning to be especially vigilant at the end where a covey might have run and skulked. Ajax came unstuck at such moments and, with a snort of recognition, would gallop on, head down, deaf to all entreaty with myself sprinting along in the rear, and flush the birds 10yd out of range. The stubbles were light relief after that and were quickly combed, but I knew where the wet dykes were and putting Ajax on a lead I crept up and peeped over the rushes in the hope of surprising a family party of mallard or teal. It was a poor day when I could not bag at least a couple by this method.

The partridges, of which greys dominated, were everywhere, springing with no warning. Suddenly an electric whirring as of a moth in a paper bag and a covey would catapult up and scatter to all points with a rusty chirrup of alarm. You had to be quick or they were off, no matter that you were off balance or tangled up in the potato haulms. It was hammers back, quick mount, pick a bird and fire. I learned to shoot at the first bird I saw having quickly found out the folly of changing once committed. In time I became quite handy and Ajax retrieved, hunted and flushed as happy as a king for all the livelong day.

Once I walked into a veritable partridge convocation and up sprang a good seventy birds in one huge pack. I got only one which towered and dropped two fields away in a field of standing corn. By fixing my eye on a single dot of a red poppy by the very spot, I walked to within one field and Ajax took off on his own and ten minutes later came slowly back with the bird. He had no dash nor style, but did everything with a ponderous and dignified slowness. He would have scored few marks in a field trial for his delivery. As for rarities, harrier, badger, death's head hawk moth, swallowtail butterfly, smew, and once, memorably a corncrake, all crossed our paths at various times, their presence unguessed at by any local naturalist.

I ate my lunch on a dyke bank in the shade, gun and bag lying beside me and Ajax sprawled on a couch of dead rushes. In the evening we found ourselves, pleasantly tired by the miles, back where we had started at my bicycle, the dew already gathering on the chrome handlebars. Suddenly it was not so warm, the sun was on the opposite horizon as red faced as I after a day spent under its smile. Dusty, tired and in slow motion we toiled home from the America, up that gruelling slope, down the high street and home, Ajax padding behind me wearily, the bag strap cutting into my shoulder with the weight of birds.

Little did I know that walking-up partridges in September would fall from fashion or that the birds themselves would become scarce or that the silly pheasant would colonise the Fens or that farms would be sold, improved, sprayed, changed, modernised and fields enlarged, or that my patrons would grow old and retire, giving way to hard, new men, or that the shooting rights might be sold to townies. At the time it was a way of life as permanent and as perennial as the grass and I could not imagine that it would ever change.

Those now secure in their shooting rights and practices would do well to bear this tale in mind, for history is often a good teacher. As for me, I learned that to shoot without a dog was little pleasure, that birds falling stone dead were as good as lost if they fell in cover or over water. Already I was tired of hanging a handkerchief on a stalk and walking round it in increasing circles until I could find the fall.

Ajax was good with the duck but his coat was not as waterproof as that of many labs. In winter he seemed to absorb and then exude the cold, a glance at him causing the most cosily wrapped companion to shiver. On and on he went, doing his stuff in his own way, slowly swimming out and as slowly coming back; in frozen-frame action emerging from the water, the duck clamped in that velvet bag which did duty for a mouth. In old age he grew rheumatic and waxed exceeding crafty at insinuating himself between the close-ranked easy chairs and bagging the best place at the fire.

Again my life moved on and I left Ajax at home for the college years. He shuffled round the village, enjoying his seventh age with dignity and extreme guile until, one day, he was hit by a speeding car and so badly injured that Mr Jackson the vet had no option but to put him down. Again tears sprang to the eyes, but so it must be with dogs, and him too we buried in the garden and I drank a stiff Scotch provided by my mother who understood about such things.

That dog and I shared an era of shooting which was not to return; our companionship during the early, learning years was one which, no matter how many expensive and highly trained dogs I might have possessed thereafter, was not to be repeated. Ajax was a good companion and fellow sportsman who enjoyed the game, was possessed of a wry sense of humour and who taught a callow youth more than he deserved.

Introduction to Field Work

GEOFFREY ARMITAGE

Geoffrey Armitage spent many of his early years in Ireland, where he encountered red setters, pointers and labradors. In 1938, starting his military career, he purchased his first English springer spaniel, and has continued to own, train and work them ever since, plus a number of black labradors.

His first direct interest in the competitive side of gundog work began nearly thirty years ago, when two of his spaniels won working tests for retrievers. Field trialling soon followed with sufficient success to maintain his enthusiasm until the present day. He started judging spaniel field trials in 1968 and has also judged retriever stakes more recently. Of particular satisfaction to him were a young springer and a young labrador, both of whom won the first field trial he ran them in.

Having left the army in 1973 he became director of the CLA Game Fair. Over the next few years he introduced the Gundog Scurry and the Gundog Pick-up which continue to this day, and also Mixed Doubles, an event for two dogs, one hunting the other retrieving.

He started writing about most aspects of gundog work for various magazines in 1965. He shoots regularly with his gundogs and picks-up in Dorset.

Control Training

Taking a young inexperienced gundog of whatever sort out in the shooting field for the first few times is a critical stage in the development of a working type which if all goes well will be a trustworthy asset for many seasons. A comparison can be made with the young soldier who has learnt the drill on the familiar barrack-square, and then finds himself in all sorts of conditions and situations on the battlefield. His reactions will depend on his own character and on the thoroughness of his early training, added to the way he is led.

Gundogs are classified in four main groups: the pointers and setters,

Complete steadiness is needed before the introduction to retrieving

'bird dogs'; the retrievers; the spaniels and the hunting, pointing and retrieving breeds. Each group has been developed over the centuries for certain purposes.

Bird dogs do not customarily retrieve shot game, indeed they are the only group which is not expected to collect the slain. Steadiness is all-important, often they have to hunt some distance from the handler and temptations like running hares or rabbits must be resisted.

Retrievers, according to the book, perform only one role though some are encountered which are prepared to work like a spaniel hunting for game to flush. I had a useful yellow labrador in Egypt nearly forty years ago which used to point quail in corn, a habit which we made full use of.

Spaniels perform two functions. Firstly, hunting to find and put up game, both furred and feathered, within range; secondly, to retrieve what has been hit to order. I repeat to order. Absolute steadiness and obedience are vital and these come under test when a bird falls close to the spaniel and proceeds to flap its wings on the ground or to run.

The HPRs, of course, are gundogs expected to perform all three functions; hunting, in open country up to a couple of hundred yards from the handler or in cover like a spaniel sometimes out of sight for short periods.

In the open he must point game and remain steady until told to flush, and finally to recover what has been shot. A dog which can do all this properly is a real pleasure.

How do you set about this vital stage in a working-dog's life? Assuming that he has mastered basic training satisfactorily, what is his outlook and his attitude to his owner? If the owner has personally laid down the basic training he or she should be able to judge the dog's intelligence, courage and confidence and his will to please. Allowance must be made if there are any doubtful points. If the basic stuff has been done elsewhere, time must be allowed for handler and youngster to get on familiar terms before taking to the shooting field.

At this point all sorts of new factors come into play. Basic training has probably taken place in the same familiar area and the youngster knows it

The dummy launcher is a useful aid, but don't overdo it

well. Out for a day's shooting it is a different story: new ground and conditions; strange people and all sorts of gundogs not previously encountered.

Different Roles

A gundog may be required to work in different ways. On a rough shoot spaniels and HPRs are in their element. There is plenty of hunting in a variety of cover, obstacles of various sorts which may not have been encountered before and a certain amount of game which may be encountered at any time.

Then there is the grouse moor, where in sparsely populated areas the bird dogs, pointers and setters, are in their element. Retrieving types can earn their colours too, both on walking days across the moor and in the more heady atmosphere when grouse are being driven over the butts. Heather takes some getting used to, it varies in height and thickness. Birds which have been wounded can tuck in on a warm still day, and it needs a retriever with experience and a good nose to locate them. The proportion of gundogs fortunate enough to be taken on grouse moors is comparatively small. Most of them gain their experience on pheasant and partridge shoots, which are a different story and vary in the sort of country they occupy and the way they are conducted and the amount of game shot.

Finally there is wildfowling where a keen courageous patient retriever can make all the difference to the bag. Varying light, sometimes working in near darkness, weeds, waterfalls and currents all affect the issue so far as the swimming dog is concerned.

Each type of shooting occasion poses different problems for the gundogs involved, and it pays to prepare them in the conditions likely to be encountered. Whatever happens, the ideal gundog is the one which keeps an eye on his handler and conforms to orders given by word of mouth, whistle or hand signal. 'Hasten slowly' is a phrase to keep in mind when it comes to taking a young gundog out shooting. The age to start this tortuous business will vary. The retriever or spaniel puppy, which has undergone six or so months basic training should be ready to progress to more dramatic occurrences by the time he is a year old. HPRs mature more slowly and need a few months more before being taken out shooting. Individual youngsters vary, even litter brothers and sisters can develop quite differently as they mature.

Hazards and Obstacles

Basic training may or may not have included encountering cattle, sheep and domestic fowl. Moorland sheep, for example, can be a temptation to the active young pointer or setter working some distance from his handler. He should be introduced to them with the handler close by. Care must be taken in the shooting field when such hazards appear. A useful springer bitch of mine

Some trainers do not allow retrievers to touch fur

spoiled her chances in a field trial when some cows gathered round the bird she was required to retrieve. She kept well clear until they were driven off.

Obstacles are another hazard which may have been encountered during early training, but a young dog may find himself up against all sorts of difficult places in the shooting field; high stone walls on grouse moors; strong, high, wire netting with an accursed barbed wire strand above the top; cattle grids; swift flowing streams. The dog should be familiarised with as many such hazards as possible early in his shooting career.

Retrieving

Retrieving is the primary task of many gundogs, and the introductory phase is all-important. To take a young dog out on a busy shoot with birds falling all round him is, as some wit put it, like taking a nun to a night-club. Much care and time are required before you can be certain that the precious animal is steady and silent, and that he has not got or developed a hard mouth.

Progressing from fur and feather-covered dummies in basic training, next comes the introduction to a cold rabbit, a pigeon or rook. Each should be retrieved once only. When the pupil is picking-up and delivering these with confidence, he can be tried on a freshly shot rabbit or bird, care being taken that there is no blood thereon. Occasionally you come across a pheasant by the side of the road which has been struck by a car. This, when cold, can be retrieved by the young dog, and a leveret which is a road casualty can be similarly employed.

When the dog is retrieving sensibly he should be taken out on ground where there are rabbits about. Take your gun: it is time to learn what it is for. A young retriever should be kept strictly at heel, in such a position that he can see forward. A spaniel may be allowed to hunt light cover in the process, but he must be brought to heel if he shows any signs of independence encouraged by the scent and presence of game. When the gun is fired and a rabbit shot, the youngster should sit and await orders. The handler walks to the target and checks it for blood while the dog stays put for two minutes or so. Then comes the order to fetch and hopefully a quick find and a speedy return to hand.

Some people prefer someone else to do the shooting while they concentrate on the pupil. This is fine if there is someone available who understands gundog work and the training stage the animal has reached, but it is not always possible to find an assistant. If you do the shooting yourself, keep the dog uppermost in your mind. Shots should be taken carefully, not too close so that the animal is tempted to run in, preferably where there is some cover so that the dog has to use his nose to find the slain.

Working at a distance – use the whistle and unmistakeable hand signals

Introduction to shot: invite a friend to help

There should be no need to use your voice while an experienced retriever is at work, but an uncertain youngster attempting his first find will benefit from some vocal encouragement. At this stage he should be kept in sight all the time and respond instantly to any directions. Here his basic training, if properly carried out, should ensure obedience and a swift delivery. Such occasions should not last long. Half an hour, one or two rabbits or pigeons shot and that should be enough. The more you attempt to do, the more likely the novice dog is to get over-excited and to display independence. Physical fitness is important but the inexperienced canine mind is likely to tire more quickly than the young body.

In time the youngster should be introduced to all sorts of game including duck and woodcock. The latter can pose problems, I recall seeing a young red setter at home in Ireland years ago advance to inspect a woodcock someone had just shot, sniff it and then lift his leg on the bird. It pays to get hold of a shot woodcock and hand it to a retrieving dog which has not encountered the bird before, encouraging him to hold on to it for a time. Then throw the bird a few yards and get the dog to fetch it. This has worked well with a number of my labradors and springers.

Running birds are another problem. The young dog should never be sent after a runner in the open and time must be allowed after it has gone into cover, out of sight. It is better to send a novice retriever for a live hen pheasant rather than a cock which may react violently when the youngster tries to pick it up. A hen is more likely to tuck in and be fairly easy to get hold of.

Every bird and animal, dead or alive, carried by a young dog should be examined for damage caused by the retriever. This is best done by placing it in the palm of the hand breast uppermost, and feeling the ribs between thumb and finger. They should be round and firm. If crushed it may be the result of a hard mouth. However, there are times when a bird is shot close in the body or it strikes a branch or wall in falling. This may cause similar damage and should not be attributed to the dog. Some people claim that novice retrieving dogs usually bite some of their first retrieves but I have not often found this to be so.

It is a moot point whether to take an experienced retriever with you on a novice's first few expeditions. Provided he is absolutely steady, it not only sets a good example to the youngster, but also can be used to carry out difficult retrieves which might overface the learner. It is not advisable to take two 'green' youngsters out together with the gun. It is hard enough to concentrate fully on one and an element of competition is liable to arise if, for example, a hare gets up close to them and proves an irresistible temptation. Fortune was on my side years ago when I was preparing a young springer for his first field trial. Hunting some roots a hare got up in front of me and set off to my right as the dog quartering the ground came towards me from that side. They met skull to skull, and that spaniel ever afterwards regarded hares as dangerous beasts. Should the worst happen and a young spaniel give chase after a hare or rabbit despite orders to the contrary, action must be taken promptly. The dog should be secured as quickly as possible and taken to the exact spot where he set off after the fur, shaken and scolded and then be made to sit there for a period. Ideally the circumstance should be repeated as soon as possible and hopefully the youngster, remembering the first indiscretion, will sit correctly as the animal departs. Praise should follow, indeed good work by a young dog in the field should always be a matter for comment.

The presentation of edible rewards in the shooting field is not to be encouraged. It is not long before the dog reckons his handler is just a portable food bin, and his mind is more on what he can get rather than his proper work.

At times there are a number of birds to be retrieved, for example at the end of a drive on a grouse moor. The veterans can be despatched to search the

Clumber spaniel working purposefully with the dummy

fall area and bring back what they find but the young first-season retrieving dog should be handled strictly to places where a bird has been accurately marked down. Otherwise the animal gets into the habit of careering about, enjoying himself hugely but acting quite independently and achieving little unless he puts a foot on a bird. Whatever the circumstances when retrieving is to be done, the dog must be in touch with his handler and ready to obey orders promptly.

Changing and Marking Birds

A fault to guard against is changing birds when retrieving. The eager youngster gathers a bird, then sees another fall. He hastens to the second, dropping the first in the process, or I have seen labradors trying to carry both birds together.

Marking falling birds needs practice to extend what has been learnt in earlier training with dummies. Cover and scent vary and even experienced dogs find it difficult to locate grouse in thick heather on a hot windless August day. Wind strength and direction affect retrieving in various ways. Some areas where birds have fallen may be screened by a wall or slope resulting in no air scent to aid the searching dog.

Spaniels and retrievers, carrying out their normal functions, are likely to get entirely different views of falling game. The retriever correctly at heel or sitting by the gun learns to watch the direction the weapon is pointing and to see the shot bird come down. The spaniel, on the other hand, may be hunting thick cover and be only able to assess the direction in which the flushed bird took off. This applies also to the HPR working in thick vegetation.

Control

Whether a young dog out in the shooting field for the first few times should be kept on a lead is a moot point. Much depends on the temperament of the creature and how he has been reacting to what has gone on. Some advise placing a cord round the neck and letting it hang loose. Its presence somehow exerts a degree of control and may avert a disastrous run-in.

An occasion some years ago concerned a young black labrador and two springers, one old and sensible the other still learning. It was the two young-sters' first big day after what I thought had been appropriate experience on rabbits and pigeons. It was down on the shoot calendar as a driven partridge day late in October so I anticipated a modest bag of about thirty brace. Not so! The shoot owner announced to the assembled guns that 'good' pheasants could be shot too. We could not take up a position well behind the guns on the first drive because a return drive was to follow immediately.

I sat my trio near an old friend in the middle of the line of guns and resolved to keep a careful eye on them. Soon the pheasants started to come over high and fast, 'good' birds all of them. The gun was shooting well and dropped half a dozen around his peg while I stood close to the dogs. Then he shot a cock pheasant which fell in the open 5yd in front of us and proceeded to flap its wings. A few seconds later off went the young labrador despite hasty vocal commands and brought the bird triumphantly to hand. What a dilemma! To punish him at this point might convey the impression that the delivery of the pheasant was wrong. It could put him off retrieving for some time, so all I could do was take the bird and sit him down. To my relief the young spaniel had behaved correctly throughout this episode. The day's bag was well over two hundred, mostly pheasants.

There was a sequel a few weeks later, when the labrador was at his first and only field trial. There was a long delay and a slow drive while we waited under the judge's eye behind a gun. Shooting was taking place further along the line but our man never raised his weapon until near the end of the drive. At last a bird came to him and he put it down flapping straight in front of us. Off went my young hope, and that was the end of that. Perhaps I should have put him on a cord on that first occasion when I realised how much was likely to be shot. He remains an outstanding retriever in the ordinary shooting field but I keep the cord dangling from his neck as he sits beside me as birds are being driven over us.

Retrieving birds from or across water is another experience for the youngster which has already done some water training. The first few duck should be dead ones floating on the surface. A lightly shot bird which can dive to evade capture is a task for an older retriever. Delivery to hand without pausing to shake the water out of his coat must be insisted on when the novice has his turn and any tendency to drop the bird discouraged.

During the introductory phases on any kind of shooting occasion it is best to err on the side of caution. Thus the young dog should not retrieve every bird or animal that is shot and certainly not those lying in the open. A trainer from Kent once told me that he had undertaken the basic training of a young golden retriever belonging to a keen shooting man and reckoned he had him ready for the field. On a Friday evening the owner appeared to collect his dog with the following day's pheasant shooting in mind.

On the Sunday morning he brought the dog back to the trainer, looking grim. 'Dog's no good,' he announced. 'Why? What happened?' 'Took him out yesterday, and halfway through the day he just seemed to pack in and would not do anything.' 'How many retrieves had he done?' asked the trainer, who held the young dog in high esteem. 'Oh, not more than sixty,' came the reply. No further comment seems necessary.

Opinions do vary about how long a young novice dog should be kept out on a shooting day, whether working or watching. A keen one can get frustrated if he sees others enjoying all the work, while he is kept tethered on a lead. The young dog should be given the chance to emulate the lucky ones at least for a period during the day. A sensible compromise is to have the young dog in action for a drive or two, and then return him to the motor car. If there is more than one beginner they can work in turn always under strict control. You must beware of any signs of independence. As the season goes on and the young dog gains experience, he may become over-confident and keen. Any such indication must be dealt with promptly and strict compliance to orders insisted upon. The wise handler out with a young animal on a big day does not carry a gun, giving his complete attention to the animal.

He will also be circumspect about the company he and his young hope keep out shooting. The dog is likely to be highly impressionable and the examples set by other strange dogs may give him all sorts of ideas, mostly highly discreditable. Take the indulgent owner with a whining dog who has become accustomed to him making a noise waiting for birds to appear over the guns. It is a major fault and a distraction to other people within earshot. Running-in to fall is tolerated in some circles, again a serious and exasperating habit, which must not be allowed to infect the young prodigy. The dog should be watched carefully if kept close to a busy line of firing guns. If there is any sign of gun-nervousness he should be taken well clear of the noise.

Hunting and Flushing

Hunting and flushing game are the primary tasks of all the groups except the retrievers. Take first the spaniel breeds, springers and cockers being the most numerous. Introducing a youngster to work with the walking gun needs care. Initially the cover need not be punishing, although in time a spaniel should be prepared to face the fierce stuff in search of game. The pace at which the line advances is important. Often a dog hunting in a line of beaters walking fast does not have time to investigate all the cover he should, and he gets in the habit of skirting in order to keep up.

On the first sessions with handler and gun there should be a certain amount of game scent to encourage the youngster. Rabbit is better than pheasant at this stage, because the latter tends to run ahead and a spaniel which begins to take a line forward, instead of quartering the ground close in front of the handler, is not covering all the places he should, and is liable to flush quarry out of shot. Not every bird or rabbit should be killed. One or two to provide rewarding retrieves will suffice. More important is the way the young dog investigates the cover, the pace he goes, the attention he pays the handler and his reaction to flush or command. These early outings should be kept short; half an hour's hard work is probably enough for a beginner.

Bird dogs are usually initiated on a grouse moor, although partridge-holding ground is also suitable. On the first hunting day it is advisable not to shoot any birds the young entry flushes until he is clearly reacting correctly. Then make sure you shoot nothing which will fall close to the dog. Here the presence of other guns helps, the handler concentrating on his dog. The youngster should beat into the wind turning as required at either flank. The handler must exercise careful control when, for example, the dog accidentally flushes birds downwind of where he is hunting or blunders into them instead of stopping after getting the scent.

Short periods of work are all that are needed and perhaps a couple of times a week on the moor. Very windy days should be avoided with a young dog in his first season. A critical matter is the bird dog's steadiness on point because it takes time for the nearest two or three guns to move into position in range. Should he cast care aside and run forward to flush without orders he must be scolded and dragged back by the neck to the spot at which he was pointing and kept there for several minutes.

Pointer-retrievers need a careful introduction to the shooting field. Prudence suggests that they should be used to hunt, point and flush game during their first season. Retrieving shot birds comes later, otherwise there is a risk that the dog will run in when a bird he has pointed and flushed to order is shot and falls temptingly close in front. A weimaraner specialist commented that a young excited dog may tend to crush a bird in its jaws. These versatile all-purpose dogs must learn about open-ground shooting like grouse moors, and also the sort of cover normally associated with spaniels, where the distance he hunts away from his handler must obviously be limited. In woodlands and brambles he should quest on a 30yd front, flushing game with energy and drive and remain steady to shot and fall until ordered to retrieve.

Picking-up

Opinions differ about the advisability of taking an inexperienced dog picking-up on a big shoot. The owner and his headkeeper want all shot game retrieved and put in the bag with the minimum fuss and delay. The retrievers are expected to cope with everything that falls and that includes strong runners in the open. If you can take an older dog as well as the novice, you should be able to fulfil requirements as a picker-up and give the youngster some selected retrieves to do. Most shooting folk appreciate the business of

One of the objects of the whole exercise: a confident retrieve in adverse conditions

introducing a novice retriever to the field, and if they are not aware of the finer points, it does them no harm to learn about them.

A German practice before a gundog is allowed to come out on a shooting day in company is to give him a test in front of judges experienced in training and working dogs. The candidate is taken out with one or two guns, made to work including retrieving pinioned duck and he has to show that he is obedient, quiet and courageous. Such a system might be applied here, especially to those hopefuls who want to try their hand at field trials.

At first sight it may appear that introducing a young gundog to the shooting scene is nothing but a mass of pitfalls and precautions. It need not be so if preliminary training has been thoroughly done, the animal has all the right characteristics and is genuinely at one with his owner. First impressions mean a good deal and the enjoyment in taking out a youngster which performs entirely to your satisfaction, and hopefully everybody else's, is tremendous. A last cautionary word; do not assume that a successful initiation ensures permanent perfection. Concentrate on the dog every time he takes the field, anticipate possible defects in behaviour and keep up the basic drills between shooting occasions.

Cassius

JOHN HUMPHREYS

I was living in Berkshire at the time, the demise of poor old Ajax still rankling, when the need for a dog reasserted itself. I was able to bag a bit of roughshooting on a small farm which also held a horse pond, much frequented by the local mallard. One bitter winter morning, just as a frosty sun was edging above the petrified twigs of the beeches, I dropped a right and left as a string of duck left the water quacking their alarm. I had risen at an unmentionable hour and undergone a long stalk and there lay my birds in the hole in the middle of the ice, both stone dead, an orange paddle waving feebly.

I was not intending to leave them. I lay down my gun, found a long branch from the edge of the wood, gritted my teeth and waded out into the water, a human ice-breaker, smashing a path as I went. My, but it was cold and the chill tide crept up my body until I felt its adder bite first on my belly, then my chest. Even then, with my long stick, the birds still lay a tantalising few feet beyond my reach. Rash young chap that I was, even I would not venture further as I felt the mud ooze and grow dangerously soft beneath my feet. I went home duckless, came back later with a pair of breast-high waders and a proper stick of gargantuan proportions, only to find that the two duck had been ruined by crows.

That was a bad experience and an advertisement for a litter of well-bred black labrador puppies in the local paper had a new wife and a keen young shooter rushing down to Lambourn, home of great horses and trainers, in order to get the pick of the litter. The bitch belonged to Mr David Cecil, the racehorse trainer and he took us into a palatial loose box where, on a layer of fresh straw and in an enclosure of bales there played as delightful a litter of eight pups as you could wish to see. There were to be no mistakes, for I had plenty of time. I chose the one which came up to me boldly, ran first to the rolled-up handkerchief which I tossed on the floor and which seemed to be in charge of the rest of them. I paid my £25 and once more I was a dog-owner.

He ate like a horse, grew apace and was, as the postman said, 'As black as the Earl of Hell's waistcoat'. He was the largest and most powerful labrador I have ever seen. He feared nothing or no one, was pretty headstrong and would fetch a bird from wherever it fell. I named him Cassius not because he had a lean and hungry look – far from it – but after the famous boxer Cassius Clay, later to become the renowned Muhammed Ali. As for cover, he forgot he was a labrador, some of which are said to be scared stiff of a stinging nettle, and thought he was a giant springer. He burst through decades-old thorn hedges, burrowed in prickles and breasted ice-locked lakes as though they were feather beds.

Some shooting invitations began to trickle in and the kind host would add, almost as an afterthought, '. . . and don't forget to bring Cassius'. Already his reputation grew. On one memorable day when shooting in the Fens during a cold snap, a pheasant was shot over the bank from where Cassius and I stood. The bird crashed down into the middle of a shallow, but frozen, lagoon of water on the river wash. A halt was called and we stood still, as good as gold and then, when nothing seemed to be happening save for a lot of shouting, we strolled up to the top of the bank to see what was what. A succession of dogs were tried at that bird. One by one they were sent out by proud owners; they'd *show them how it was done, but one by one they felt the ice giving beneath their feet, lost confidence the further they ventured from shore and one by one came creeping back to stern admonishments.*

Roger the keeper was not going home without that bird, lying there in full view. 'Fetch Cassius,' he called and, ever ready, we tried our hand. I need not have worried for the old monster went ploughing through, not over, the ice, bursting a channel of floating sheets of the stuff, snatched the bird and came galloping back, not by the path he had just made and which was the easy route, but contemptuously crashing another, fresh pathway as if to show the rest just how easy it was. Ever after on that shoot, they would shout 'Where's Cassius?' when there was the call for any extrovert canine feat or impossible bird to be fetched.

I was exceedingly proud of him and during our best spell, I reckoned from my game book that he had retrieved a thousand duck in five years, together with unrecorded pheasants and other game. He was no good at a peg as he was the type of character who wanted to get involved in the action. It was then that he began to show a change of personality for the worse.

I put it down to the coke boiler. At home he slept in a box in the large kitchen not far from the solid-fuel boiler, an awful old thing which either flared up, grew red hot and used all the fuel or sulked sullenly and went out, whereupon I was obliged to take out all the coke by hand in order to give it a fresh start. The trick was to dampen it down just enough to keep it glowing, prevent it going out overnight and also prevent it burning out. I grew fairly cunning at this and could usually get it about right.

One night I was awoken by a ghastly, unearthly screaming and moaning from below. Down I rushed and on entering the kitchen was immediately aware of a bad sensation in my throat, nothing I could smell, but a creeping poison seemed to be stifling my very breath in my lungs with the power of an invisible hand on my throat. On the floor lay Cassius, stretched out, the matting covered with vomit and urine. I opened the back door, grasped him by the scruff and dragged him out; he was far too big to carry. In the garden I heaved him to his feet; he tottered a bit but slowly regained consciousness and staggered about until he had all but recovered. I have no doubt that he had been a victim of carbon-monoxide poisoning. He was a dog who never complained, was impervious to pain and only in extremis would he have cried out. Two weeks later exactly the same thing happened, but this time I complained to my landlord, telling him that he would have dead people as well as a dead dog on his hands unless he did something about the stove; a new one was fitted and the problem seemed to be cured.

Cassius was never the same again. A mean streak had developed, caused I am sure by oxygen starvation and brain damage during those two close calls with the gas. No longer could he be trusted. He fought with dogs on shoots and being so strong he was rarely bested, sometimes taking on the whole pack at once. When this happened on a laden gun's trailer it was a fairly fraught occasion with people leaping up the walls and sticking their legs in the air to avoid being bitten. Clearly that could not continue and I took to leaving him at home after some fellow sportsmen dropped fairly strong hints that I, but not he, was welcome. I took him when I felt I could keep him away from other dogs. On one such occasion I had shot a hare, Cassius had retrieved it and at the end of the drive the beaters came walking past the pegs. One beater bent down to pick the hare, at which Cassius turned in a flash and bit him clean through the thickest part of his hand.

He took to growling savagely as I fed him, until I was obliged to adopt the absurd procedure of putting down his bowl and pushing it along the ground to him with a long pole, rather as one might feed a lion in a cage. Thereafter, one by one, he bit most of the family but always I made the grave error of justifying it saying that the dog had a good reason. I asked the advice of friends who urged me to get rid of him, but it was not the advice I wanted to hear and the evil day was deferred. He was my only dog, and was still an amazing bag-filler and worker.

The error of my weakness was brought home to me in a manner which still makes me shudder when I recall it. Digging in the garden I forked out an old golf ball. Along the ground it rolled coming to rest between Cassius' mighty paws where he lay snoozing in the sun. The dog leaped up, picked up the ball, threw it, played with it and scampered after it like a ten-week old puppy. Then again he lay down with his nose on it between his paws. My small son Peter, then aged two, came toddling up, stooped down and like a man in a nightmare unable to shout a warning or take action to prevent the inevitable, I saw him bend to pick up the ball. Cassius gave a deep growl, then a roar and as quick as light, snatched the child by his upper arm, picking him up and shaking him as a terrier does a rat. I raised the digging fork above my head and brought it down with all my might on the dog's back shattering the stout handle as I did so. He dropped the lad and skulked off to his kennel.

To cut a painful story short, the boy had a compound fracture of the humerus and spent a difficult fortnight with his mother in hospital. Had the dog, as well he might, grabbed him round the neck instead of the arm it would have been a different story and all my fault. Home from hospital I called the dog who came out all wagging tail and delight at being taken for a car ride, his fearful crime already forgotten. I could barely look at him for he had let me down so badly and betrayed my trust. 'Get in the car,' was all I could say. We went straight to the vet where he was put down and so great was his stamina that it took two injections to finish him. Oddly enough I even shed a tear at his passing for we had had some good times together in his early days, he was still a fairly young dog, but he was not the little chap we had bought with such hope back in that stable in Lambourn.

It is a human's world not a dog's and the rules, sadly enough, are ours. Dogs which transgress, however logical to them their behaviour may seem, have no escape. Now older and wiser I would not have let things go so far. Every dog, they say, is allowed one bite, but that should be warning enough and, hard though it may be, strong action at that time might prevent a fearful tragedy later.

Cassius was another phase in my dog-owning life. He too taught me much, some of it painful, but he was a chapter in a shooting dog-owner's story and we must learn to accept the bad news as well as the good as being integral parts of the same tale.

The Beating Line

JACK DAVEY

Jack Davey was born in 1931 and was brought up in a remote Norfolk village between Diss and Thetford, close to some of the best Norfolk shooting estates. His childhood was surrounded by dogs, guns, ferrets and nets and a complete rural life. His weekends and school holidays were spent pursuing rural activities, mainly dogging, shooting and fishing. He was still at school when he first joined the beating line, and a few years later started beating with dogs and picking-up.

In 1957 he bought his first pedigree gundog, an English springer spaniel; in fact he went to buy another terrier and was persuaded by the kennel maid to buy a spaniel – a lucky stroke of fate. After training the dog and shooting over him, he decided to try him in a field trial and was awarded a certificate of merit in his first trial. From that day, he was bitten by the field trial 'bug' and is still as enthusiastic about trials today, some thirty years later. Although he keeps retrievers in his kennel he rarely trials them. As he puts it: 'There's so much more to spaniel work and the trials are more exciting – you're never quite sure what's going to happen next!'

Jack has judged trials and tests throughout the British Isles for over twenty-five years. He has judged the Spaniel Championship Stakes three times and for several years was the captain of the England Gundog Team for the International Gundog Match. He is Chairman of the Westward Gundog Society and serves on other Field Trial Society committees. In the sixties and seventies he exported some successful spaniels to the USA. His famous FTCh Wivenwood Fofo produced Wivenwood Willie, the dog that became an American National Field Trial Champion when only eighteen months old, creating a record.

His two remaining ambitions in the gundog world are to win the Spaniel Championship (his best so far is third place) and to judge the Championship Stakes once more and thus create an individual record.

'A springer – the commando of the shooting field – always ready, willing and able to tackle anything with enthusiasm'

Taking the high ground, with a dog as the perfect companion

(Opposite) *Labrador sits steadily at the peg while the spectator takes avoiding action*

Clever springer retrieves a drake mallard, ignoring the decoys

'Then there is the grouse moor, where in sparsely populated areas the bird dogs, pointers and setters, are in their element'

An Introduction to the Beating Line

I was a schoolboy when I served my apprenticeship in the beater's line on an estate in the Thetford area on the Norfolk/Suffolk borders. The few shillings I received for a Saturday's beating stood me in good stead in the school tuck shop for the following week and put me on a level with those boys whose parents were better off. It was during those austere years just after World War II and times were difficult. Formal driven shooting had been stopped 'for the duration of the war' as had so many other things. During the years just after the war no one thought that shooting would ever be able to return to its former excellence what with increased costs, in particular wages, and the lack of resources available. But within a few years keepers were back in position and with the advent of syndicate shoots things were soon on the way up.

My recollection of those early days was that beating seemed to be a somewhat regimented business – a spill over from the war no doubt – as some keepers were ex-servicemen, sergeant-majors I would think, and the majority of guns were officers either still serving or 'demobbed' after war service. As a beater you had to be fully alert and instantly responsive to all commands. A 'straight line' meant a straight line and if the left flank was required to 'lead' then everyone on the left flank followed the instruction keeping an eye on the man either side. If you were required to 'hold it' then you stopped but those sticks had to be tapping all the time until the next order was rapped out. No one, especially the youngsters, wanted to incur the wrath of the keeper as you could be sent home there and then.

After some forty years I can still remember vividly an occasion when, as an enthusiastic youngster, the beating line was nearing the end of a drive. There was a good stream of pheasants flushing in front of the stops and I had slipped forward quickly under the cover of some rhododendron bushes just a few yards to see the sport. I thought I wouldn't be seen but I heard the beat keeper shout, 'What's that man doing out of line?'. Then I heard my father's reply, 'It's the boy, he wants to see some of the shooting,' to which the keeper replied, 'He's not here to see the shooting, he's paid to provide the shooting.' At the end of the day, when I held out my hand to take my pay, I was told in no uncertain terms, 'Now then laddie, when I say keep in line I expect you to keep in line, no nipping forward to see the shooting. If you want to keep coming here you will do as I say.' This worried me at the time, but in retrospect I am sure there was a twinkle in the keeper's eye when he said it. I never disobeyed again and I don't to this day. This training ground has stood me in good stead all my beating life.

The other thing I remember well, is that there were no dogs in the beating line, other than those with keepers and they were all retrievers. They were kept strictly at heel and never allowed to hunt. Most of the guns had a dog, usually a retriever, and there were pickers-up with dogs behind the line of guns. As a boy I had cross-bred terriers, so cross-bred they could be considered more of the Heinz 57 type, for catching rats about farmyards, when cornstacks were threshed out in the spring and, of course, for catching rabbits, especially in harvest fields. All before the introduction of the combine harvester and before the advent of myxomatosis in this country.

A few years after going out to work I became interested in gundogs and soon afterwards I started field trialling. Because of 'myxie' the ubiquitous rabbit had virtually disappeared and was now a rare species in the countryside. My own personal shooting was a bit of wildfowling or duck shooting, pigeon shooting and an occasional pheasant. Not really sufficient to experience dogs for trialling, so I was now looking to get my spaniels amongst more game to give them the experience I felt was necessary for field trials, especially steadiness to flush and retrieving practice. Due to my father's influence with the keepers and my previous work as a beater, I was able to take my dogs to the same estate and use them in the beater's line, with the odd drive to do some straight picking-up. My instructions were to hunt them until near to flushing points and then keep them into heel. No way were my Norfolk keeper friends going to risk a dog out of hand in the beater's line at a flushing point putting up a hundred pheasants at one go, when what was wanted was a steady stream, tapped out by beaters tapping their sticks against trees. But it wasn't long before they realised that I had reasonable control over my dogs and could be trusted.

On the Sunday morning, following a Saturday's shooting, I would go out with the keepers to help with the final pick-up and I remember that guns were carried by them. This was good experience for my trial spaniels as often a 'pricked' bird would be shot which gave them the full spaniel sequence of work, hunt, find, flush, remain steady, mark and retrieve.

Dogs: Help or Hindrance?

During the last twenty-five years we have witnessed a great deal of change in the shooting field, particularly in the area of organised shooting. There are still a few great shooting estates that have shooting parties with all invited guests, but unfortunately they are now in the minority. Because of the economics of running a shoot the syndicate shoot is the modern concept. Commercial shoots, as they are known, have come on the scene, much to the disgust of some, but nevertheless they are here to stay. There are some very successful shoots that are run on the lines of a farmers' co-operative where farmers pool their land and run the shoot with a part-time keeper, probably one of their workers. Then there is the do-it-yourself shoot where a group of people acquire some land and each put

Well controlled spaniels will deal with cover that the average beater will skirt round

in some effort towards controlling predators and rearing a few pheasants. With the modern indoor equipment pheasants are easier to rear and with release pens, electric fences and hopper feeding they can be successfully introduced into woodlands during the summer and provide good sport in the autumn and winter.

The present-day financial pressures and the need for shoots to be economically viable has meant that dogs have gradually become more and more valuable in the beating line. A man with a good, steady, reliable hunting dog is more than equal to three beaters just wielding sticks. A good hunting dog quartering his ground properly, can cover 15–20yd on either side of his handler and will miss very little, certainly less than beaters with sticks, unless they are only a few yards apart. A good dog will hunt his ground very thoroughly whatever the cover, more thoroughly than beaters who, if not closely supervised, tend to skirt round pieces of thick difficult cover. Also beaters have to rely on their eyes and sticks to find and present game, they haven't the nose for it like a dog. However, dogs can be too thorough for some people. Some years ago I remember asking a keeper on a well-known large estate why there were no dogs in his beaters' line. His reply was that dogs, particularly spaniels, were far too efficient and he and his employer didn't want all the birds up on one day. They felt that some should slip through the net and be available for another day as well as acting as a stabilising force to help settle down those birds that escaped being shot and eventually found their way back to their home wood. Those of you who are spaniel enthusiasts will understand.

Looking at the economics of it all, as has been said, one man and a good dog can cover the ground more effectively than three beaters. So with a little bit extra on top of beater's pay for the dog man, the wages of two beaters can be saved. This saving can be multiplied as often as you like throughout the beaters' line. Dogs are also more efficient than beaters at finding dead and wounded game from a previous drive, another valuable asset.

There are times when the keeper might consider that there are a few minus points as far as dogs are concerned. Wind direction plays an important part on how a dog treats his ground and with a following wind he will often strike scent and push in to cover at birds only to flush them back again over the beaters' line or out across the flanks rather than towards the guns. This is something that is almost impossible to control. Then there is, of course, the occasional dog which does get out of hand and takes the line of a running pheasant right into the flushing point and the lot are up in one go. The guns get one double shot and the drive is over. Usually this means

A bold leaper has some advantages

a very happy dog, a very red-faced handler and a very irate keeper! So the important point is that the dog must be absolutely steady and responsive to command, particularly the stop whistle.

Weighing up the pros and cons, there is no doubt, at least in my mind (and in a number of other minds) that a dog is an asset in the beaters' line. Many shoots today, perhaps it would be correct to say the majority of shoots, take advantage of dogs in the beaters' line. I know of one shoot that employs a complete team of beaters with dogs. The handlers are paid a bonus over the top of the usual beater's pay for the locality. This, of course, is very acceptable to the dog-handlers and is a great saving in the budget item for beaters in the finances of the shoot.

What Type of Dog?

It could be suggested that any dog in the beating line is better than no dog at all, or that any dog that will hunt cover will do. But it is not quite that simple and there is a lot more to it than just hunting. The dog must be a natural hunter with plenty of stamina to go for several hours in a day, so he must be from one of the breeds which enjoy hunting for hunting's sake, not just on scent but to find scent. He must be fully trained which means from a breed, or more correctly, a strain of a breed which is biddable and responsive. He must be soft mouthed so that there is no damage to any bird that he may be required to pick. There must be no inclination to fight other dogs as there will be times when handlers and dogs are crammed into a vehicle like sardines in a tin. There must not be the slightest hint of whining or yapping. He will need to be a dog with plenty of initiative but accept readily to have his initiative channelled in the right direction, when necessary, by his handler by whistle and hand signal. He must be able to jump, work in water and retrieve from it. Finally he should be able to work with all types of game, including ground game. To sum up, he must be fully trained, under good control and an experienced all-rounder, but nevertheless, hunting must be his strong point. You may think I have overstated the job of a dog in the beaters' line but, at times, it is quite amazing what will be asked of you, especially between drives and at the end of the day. It is not only the dogs that need stamina but also their handlers.

Whether you join a formal driven shoot or a small do-it-yourself shoot, controlled hunting will be the main task. On the larger shoot the day will be directed by keepers with plenty of beaters without dogs in the line, but on smaller shoots most of the beaters will have dogs. On the small syndicates and do-it-yourself shoots good hunting dogs will be more valuable because of the limited finances available to pay beaters. Often the beaters are made

The English springer spaniel is popular with beaters on lowground shoots

up of family or friends of the guns and sometimes guns take turns, that is, they have one drive in the beaters' line and then take up position at a stand. So we come to the conclusion that whatever class of shoot you attend, dogs will be considered invaluable for finding and flushing game and play a useful and productive part in the beaters' line which will improve the sport for the guns and will increase the bag at the end of the day. Also they will find wounded game which might otherwise have been lost and more importantly, from the humane aspect, prevent suffering.

On most shoots game can hide away in a great variety of cover and have to be found and flushed forward over the guns. The cover can be as simple as a field of roots which is not too punishing for dogs or beaters and almost any dog will hunt it reasonably well. Here the hunting pattern is important as game can be missed easily in something like sugar-beet if the dogs haven't a close symmetrical quartering pattern. Similarly, in bracken and heather on heathland and moorland, a good pattern is important. Hedgerows are more punishing to dogs and difficult for the handlers because the dogs tend to pull forward along the line of the hedge on the scent of game. Areas of bramble and scrub have to be dealt with as does woodland which often has dense bramble as underlying cover. This is much more difficult and it needs a hard-going, persistent hunting dog to keep working in these conditions for any length of time. Reed beds and rushes all have to be tackled by beaters and dogs. On some shoots it is quite possible that all the various types of cover may be encountered in one day.

Bearing all this in mind the dog that springs to mind for a day in the beaters' line, to take on anything, is one of the spaniel breeds. My first choice would be a springer – the commando of the shooting field – always ready, willing and able to tackle anything with enthusiasm. For generations, indeed centuries, they have been bred for hunting and finding game. In the days long before the advent of the shotgun, spaniel-type dogs were used for finding and flushing game for hawking. Also a similar type of dog, maybe with some pointing or setting qualities as an added attribute, was used to find and set game so that a large net could be drawn over the dog and the quarry.

In more modern times, with the introduction of the shotgun, all these qualities are still required and have been improved on to bring about our present-day spaniel with his hard hunting, cover-facing ability enhanced by speed and style. Separated out during the nineteenth century were the larger hunting dogs with their pointing and setting abilities and with selective breeding, the pointers and setters have evolved as we know them today. These larger, wider-ranging dogs are used mainly on the hill and upland shoots where vast areas of moorland have to be covered. Although spaniels may be seen, the favourite dogs are the pointers and setters. Their quartering pattern is several times wider than the average spaniel and therefore much more effective and efficient on large areas of land where game is sparse.

I am sure that some will argue that retrievers can be used successfully in the beaters' line, effectively finding and flushing game and then after the drive can be used to help with the pick-up. I have yet to see a retriever that can hunt cover like a good spaniel. Let's face the facts, retrievers came to our shooting field about one hundred and fifty years ago at the time *battue* or driven shooting was reaching its heyday and their job was picking up large numbers of game after it was shot, and not producing game to shoot. Retrievers have been developed and bred along these lines ever since. They are not the best of dogs for facing thick punishing cover, they are not built for it and they haven't been bred for it.

So our first choice of dog for the beaters' line is one of the spaniel breeds, preferably the English springer spaniel, renowned for his versatility and adaptability, being particularly suitable for those who can only keep one dog. He can take on anything required, hunting, retrieving, working in

Beaters' dogs should be under perfect control at all times

water and as a family pet. An important point to consider is that it is easier to turn one of the spaniel breeds into a no-slip retriever than it is to change a retrieving breed into a good hunting dog.

Requirements in the Beating Line

To work a dog in the beating line is not just turning up at a shoot with a dog and joining the line where it suits you best. It is a serious matter and the job has to be done properly. You will receive some reward, either in money or in kind, sometimes both and, of course, a great deal of job satisfaction. Whilst you may consider that you and your dog are going to enjoy yourselves, please bear in mind that you are there to provide a service and must follow the directions of the keeper and respect the wishes of the guns. Don't become too full of your own importance because you have a dog and think that other beaters with sticks only, are lesser mortals. You are not indispensable and the shoot can survive without you.

There is nothing special about training a dog for work in the beaters' line. Train the dog as you would for shooting or trials. Aim for the highest possible standards and if you fall short you will still have a useful and acceptable dog. Teach him to hunt cover with a regular quartering pattern, always keeping within gunshot. I would suggest no more than 20–25yd either side of the handler and no more than 15–20yd out in front. This will vary according to scenting conditions and wind direction. Even though you will be using your dog mainly to push pheasants forward to guns, there will be times when you will want him for your own personal shooting and also when there are guns walking-up in the beaters' line, when hunting out of range would be futile.

The whistle will be the main form of control. One thing that will be different is that it will not be possible for the dog to drop to every flush or shot. On many large shoots he would never get off his backside for long because of the number of birds being flushed and the number of shots being fired, and it would be just a matter of stop, start, stop. But it will still be important that he drops to whistle – one blast, as usual, so that you can stop him at any time. Also he must come in immediately to the whistle using lots of short blasts or pips. Turning when quartering will also be helpful if he is boring out too much to one side and this can be done by two pips on the whistle and soon comes very naturally to the dog if he has been taught to come in on lots of pips on the whistle.

Chasing must be strictly controlled. This will be easy providing the dog is fully responsive to the stop whistle and, of course, is in view of the handler. A dog chasing forward after a rabbit or running pheasant would go right through a flushing area and have all the birds airborne together and spoil the drive. Walking to heel will be essential and there will be times when this will be required either by the handler anticipating trouble, or when the keeper requires the beaters' line to move steadily forward repeatedly stopping and starting according to the flow of birds from the drive towards the guns.

Near the end of a drive complete concentration is required in a hunting dog so that whistle control can be applied to prevent him from dashing forward out of the beaters' line to the guns, snatching up a pheasant and bringing it back into the wood. This can annoy guns, especially those with dogs and can, of course, upset the picking-up after the drive. The dog that is really annoying is the one that loses his head completely, rushes out, picks up a bird and halfway back sees another one shot, drops the one he has and dashes off for the other and continues to do this several times, moving all the marked-down birds around and confusing the pick-up after the drive. It can be very embarrassing to witness your dog doing this and eventually finishing up having a tug of war on a dead cock pheasant with a big black labrador belonging to one of the guns. It is at this point you may wish that you were a beater with just a stick.

The Keeper's Objectives on a Shooting Day

The keeper's main objective on a shooting day is to provide good sport for the guns. The aim, by careful management of the beaters' line, is to provide high birds in a steady flow in the right direction. The beaters' job is to move the birds forward, preferably to flushing points, and then get them airborne in a steady stream to give the guns a chance to shoot and then reload. It is a carefully planned and executed operation and needs the fullest co-operation of all concerned responding implicitly to the keeper's instructions. Beaters using sticks to beat the cover out can only reach so far but those with dogs can reach much further. Hence the greater value to the keeper of a beater with a dog. But this value can depreciate rapidly if things go wrong. Remember that the keeper can control the actions of the beaters with sticks but can do little about the dogs in the line and will expect the dog-handlers to listen to his instructions and interpret them and get the dogs to respond accordingly – woe betide you if you can't!

Some Problems

So far the prospect of dogs in the beaters' line seems not only very worthwhile but straightforward; however, I can assure you, from bitter experience, that there are problems.

Dogs and beaters wait for the drive to begin

I use the beaters' line as a training ground for the young dogs I intend to run in trials and I have to be very careful not to spoil them by putting them in at the 'deep end' by giving them tasks that they are not ready to undertake. So if you are keen on trials plan your work for your dogs carefully and I usually cover myself by having an old, over the top, dog with me to take on those jobs the young dog is not really ready for. One thing that is difficult in the beaters' line is that there is little or no chance of retrieving. Therefore I occasionally pick-up at a drive to give the dogs some retrieving experience, but even so, this is not proper spaniel work because it is disjointed – all hunting and no retrieving and then all retrieving and no hunting. With constant beating they get sloppy at stopping to flush and, of course, don't bother to watch birds away as they are not shot until they get to the guns. Dropping to shot is another aspect of good spaniel work which also tends to slip although I must say that most dogs, when in the beaters' line, cannot be expected to drop to shot as there is constant shooting some distance away. Usually they will drop to shot as soon as a gun is with them and the shot is fired at a pheasant flushed by them.

Often when using a dog in the beaters' line pricked birds and runners from previous drives will be picked, a valuable piece of work from the shoot's point of view and from the humane angle, but it can unsteady dogs and encourage them to peg unshot game. I find it impossible to get over to a dog that he can chase and catch one bird and not another. Some dogs eventually do learn that there are birds with a blood scent that can be chased and caught and brought into hand, but let's face it, we as mere humans cannot always discern the difference. After a season in the beaters' line dogs can get very clever at pegging game (catching unshot game). It is amazing how well a dog can catch a pheasant that is a little slow in moving out of cover but is it a pricked bird or has the dog become a little too clever by experience?

Not all keepers show enough consideration towards their beaters with dogs. I would go as far as saying that there are some who don't fully appreciate good dog work. There are some keepers who will ask for the impossible. When driving in a large field of roots or kale, the keeper may suggest that the dogs can do as they like as they will do no harm. Maybe no harm to the drive but what about the harm to the dog? A dog cannot be expected to know that he can run wild in one drive, especially something like kale where he can chase up and down the drills and flush a bird a hundred yards forward and on return get on to another and so on, and in the next drive that he is wanted to work like a field-trial champion with a perfect pattern and within close range.

There is also a tendency for some keepers to put the dog men in that part of the line with the most impenetrable of cover. The sort of cover that the average beater will not, or cannot, get through and will have to skirt around. His instruction is usually to let the dogs hunt out the blackthorn or the rhododendrons. Again there is nothing more ruinous to a hard-going spaniel than having half an acre of rhododendrons to himself. I tend to battle through with the dog just to try and keep some sort of control. It can be a strenuous operation and usually, because of the immense task of getting through myself, I lose control of the dog and he ends up chasing and flushing birds well out of normal range. Another difficulty is the speed at which the beaters' line moves. If the line is made up of all beaters with dogs then there is no problem, but if the majority of the line is made up of beaters with sticks only, then the speed is usually far too fast for dogs to hunt out their beats thoroughly. Let's face it, however fast your spaniel is, for him to hunt 20yd each side of you and to investigate all cover thoroughly, is a slower job than a beater with a stick covering a few yards either side of him.

Some keepers will insist that the members of the beating line are equally spaced irrespective of whether they have dogs or not. This means that there will be times when a dog will hunt in front of the beater, on either side of his handler, a complete duplication of effort. Often a dog will be investigating a piece of cover around a beater's feet and he will continue to shout 'hie, hie, hie' and thrash the cover above the dog's back. This can be a little off-putting to most dogs but especially to a youngster. When spacing the line the keeper and the beaters should know that they should leave extra beating space for the dogs to cover.

Beaters are generally far too vociferous when birds flush. I do not think there is any need for the shouting that goes on when birds get up. 'Hies' and 'ahs' and 'over on the right' etc are so unnecessary. The guns are looking and listening and should be able to discover that a bird is coming towards them. This shouting and waving of arms and sticks can be very unsettling and can excite some dogs. Mind you, the problems are not all in the lap of the dog-handlers. Keepers have problems as well with dogs in the line. There are those which get out of control and hunt too far forward and promote those multiple flushes. When there is a following wind then there is a tendency for dogs to go forward and gather a piece of ground and hunt it on to the wind thus flushing birds towards the beaters' line and away from the guns. Then there are those dogs that get ultra-efficient at pegging unshot game that should have been pushed forward to the guns. But despite these few drawbacks, dogs are a greater benefit than they are a hindrance in the beaters' line.

How to Get Your Dog into the Beating Line

To get your dog into the beating line is not easy because a keeper is not going to let anyone onto his shoot if he doesn't know them and especially so with a dog. If he is having difficulty in getting sufficient beaters he may welcome you but he will want a personal recommendation from someone like a gun or one of the beaters already attending the shoot. If you are already beating without a dog then there should be no problem in convincing your keeper that you could do a better service for him with a dog. If not, then get yourself established as a normal beater for a season or two and then ask if you can bring your dog. You will have to convince the keeper that the dog has all the good qualities necessary for the job. Please make sure that he is *capable* of doing the job, can hunt cover thoroughly, is under perfect control, can retrieve and is not hard mouthed. Above all, that he is free from chasing and does not give tongue.

If you do get established on a shoot, always keep in mind that whilst you play an important part in the day's events, you are incidental to the day's activities and that it is organised for the benefit of the guns and not for you and your dog. They 'pay the piper' through the keeper and therefore he calls 'the tune'.

At the End of the Day

At the end of the day the bag will be laid out and you will feel satisfied that you have contributed to a successful and enjoyable day. The guns will have had plenty of good sport and the keeper will feel rewarded for the months of preparation and hard work that have preceded the day's shooting.

Before setting off for home check that your dog is all right, that he is dry enough to travel and has no injuries. It is amazing how dogs can ignore injuries during the excitement of the day's work, only to go very lame after the day's work is done and you will find something like a huge blackthorn stuck in a pad. After you arrive home check again, feel for thorns and the like still in pads and in the front half of the body. Remove all the burrs and sticky buds from the coat, particularly the ears, and the feathering on the legs and tail, as these are favourite places. Again dogs seem to ignore them during the day but are very irritated by them when they try to rest. Carefully look for cuts and gashes caused by barbed wire, one of the most vicious of hazards for hard-going hunting dogs that there are in the countryside. Make sure that the dog is comfortable, warm, fed and watered before you see to your own personal needs. Remember a dog cannot tell you or ask you and you have to read the animal's signals – something you will discover by experience.

Look after your dog, he is a valuable piece of equipment, a hard-working companion who asks less of you than you do of him. Most good dogs will give their all in a day in the shooting field. I have known many a dog to work himself to the point where he hasn't sufficient energy left to jump into the car.

What more can I say other than I wish you luck and hope you have as many enjoyable and satisfying days in the beating line as I have over the past forty or so years. Good luck and good hunting!

Tender Loving Care
for Gundogs

BILL MELDRUM

Bill Meldrum is one of the most experienced and highly regarded practical gundog men in the country. He spent nineteen years as head dog-trainer on the Sandringham Estate before being promoted five years ago to head keeper. Such a prestigious job on one of the most famous sporting estates in the world is no mean responsibility, for it runs to some 20,000 acres of which 18,000 are fully keepered in the old-fashioned way with no rearing but a keen adherence to the traditional skills of vermin control and habitat improvement.

Bill currently has twenty-two dogs in kennels, mostly labradors but some springer spaniels. Many of them are owned and worked by members of the Royal Family. His most famous dog was the renowned Sandringham Sidney, the only dog I know who had a film made about him. The fame of this noted champion and larger than life character should not disguise the fact that all the dogs at Sandringham are trained to the highest of standards. Bill is greatly encouraged by the fact that his employers share with him a devotion to gundogs and a dedication to preparing them to their maximum potential.

Bill has made a special study of dog welfare in the widest sense and it is to that subject that he devotes his contribution to this book.

There are many reasons why it is right and proper to take good care of your dogs. A dog is a good and loyal servant, a living and breathing mammal and home comforts and proper care are quite as important to him as to his master or mistress. To keep a dog inadequately housed, improperly fed and

A homemade kennel which incorporates some useful features

exercised only at the owner's whim, is a poor reflection on that owner and also will not allow the dog to perform at anything like his best and will almost guarantee illness in later life and a premature retirement from the field. Too many dogs, I feel, are treated as inanimate tools, there when wanted to work on a hard runner, but put in the car and forgotten while the owner retires to the warmth and comfort of a meal in the pub after shooting.

The Kennels

I have twenty-two dogs here at Sandringham at the moment, the number varies as circumstances dictate. We take a pride in our kennels and runs and you will see no mess or chewed bones or dirt in the vicinity. Good dogs deserve the best. All the kennels are standard size with a run of 8ft × 5ft and an inside area of 5ft × 5ft. In that sleeping compartment there is a raised bed, essential to avoid draughts, and this we line not with wood shavings, but with wood wool which is changed regularly. On no account should you use straw which quickly becomes soiled, spreads itself over the whole area and harbours mites and other parasites as well as harmful dust. Blankets also quickly grow smelly and need too regular changing to be of practical use. Any bedding which holds moisture from the dog's coat is to be avoided. How would you like to sleep in your bed when you had just got out of the bath and had not dried yourself? As an extra, a luxury which I do not begrudge, we have infra-red lights suspended over the bedding area. These may be turned on at will so that a wet dog may be dried gradually without the application of direct heat and in this way it is saved from the aches and pains which afflict many working dogs in later life.

The base of the whole kennel area is concrete with a sloping runnel to take away the water. A surface like this may be hosed down easily or sluiced with a bucket of water with disinfectant in it so that the run may be kept clean and hygienic. In the run itself we have a second raised area of boarding, for it is not good for dogs to lie out on concrete for long periods. They wear their joints and concrete is essentially a cold surface and not comfortable. The platform is a few inches off the ground and made of smooth, planed wood. A recycled pallet is not good enough, for the wood is rough and harsh on a dog's skin. This platform should not be fixed down but should be made to lift easily in order to sweep and wash underneath it. Such places are a collecting ground for shed hairs and other litter, all of which can harbour germs. The

An ideal open run/kennel combination

Stout weldmesh is needed for the run

platform and indeed the open side of the run should always face south in order to gain most benefit from the sunlight and to offer as much protection as possible from the north and east winds which, in this part of the country, can be especially bitter.

As for the mesh, we use 2in × 2in builders' weldmesh, 6ft high. This is high enough to prevent dogs from leaping out, although there have been odd cases of a dog after a bitch in season being able to scale it. This mesh is usually in mild steel but if you can get the galvanised equivalent it has the obvious advantage of not rusting and needs little or no maintenance. Failing that, you can always get steel mesh and paint it, but you will find that a surprisingly laborious job which requires rather more paint than you would have guessed.

All the posts and woodwork should be painted in creosote, nasty stuff to use but it prevents the dogs chewing at the posts which, when bored (a thing I try to avoid, of course) they are likely to do. Woodwork should be treated every year, for creosote quickly loses its power. It is also possible to buy metal feet for wooden posts. Drive in the metal box and insert the post. The metal only is below ground and it is treated with anti-corrosion paint. Thus when the post eventually needs replacing, you simply slip a new post into the box with no laborious hole digging or struggling to remove the rotted stump.

The runs are half roofed; that is to say the roof extends half way along so that the dog may be outside and still in the dry. There is more than one school of thought on this matter, some preferring runs to be entirely roofed, some preferring no roof at all. We have hit on a compromise here which seems to work well enough.

Some dog-handlers have strong views that working dogs are not pets and should not be allowed in the house. I disagree with those who hold that opinion insisting that their dogs should be treated as Spartan warriors and

left out in harsh conditions in the bitterest of winters, even when the dog is old and at the end of his working life. I can see no harm in having a dog indoors, for many shooting folk with one dog might not have the room outside for a kennel and run such as I have described. However, it is important that a dog indoors has a territory to himself which is sacred, even if it is a basket in the scullery or a corner of the kitchen. Such a thing is important to dogs so that they know they can escape to the privacy of their own particular corner where they will not be disturbed or molested. If there are small children in the house, they must be taught to respect the desire of the dog to keep himself to himself now and then and they must not pester him.

One of the great advantages of the indoor dog is that he has regular contact with humans. I cannot stress too strongly how important this is. To be regularly in human company builds up a strong bond between dog and handler, teaches the dog good manners and consideration and is in every way desirable. The main problem of dogs left out in kennels for twenty-three and a half hours a day with no human company nor sight nor sound of their handler, is that they are harder work when it comes to entering the mixed company of the shooting field. That is no way to treat a loved companion.

Exercise

Another vexed question is the daily exercise routine. Elsewhere in this book you will find explanations of training procedures so I will mention only what is essential. I am a strong believer that the man/dog relationship is therapeutic and beneficial to both. I know of several high-powered business folk who spend their time in the great pressure of London commerce who find the few minutes spent out with the dog, even if it is in a town park, are very valuable. It recharges their batteries and allows them to unwind. As for time, all you need is a minimum of ten minutes in the morning and as much again at night. This may be done in the garden if it is large enough or on a public footpath where the dog may romp and open his bowels so that he can spend the rest of the day in comfort. Dogs are happy sleeping for very long periods and can also indulge in intense activity when called on, much as their wild ancestors did. It is handy if your dog can have access to the garden when you are out all day in case he is caught short. In this case, make sure that your garden is fully dog proofed with fence or wall and be careful to leave the gate shut. A dog roaming the streets is nothing short of a liability.

We are fortunate here at Sandringham with such a great and varied terrain on the estate to provide dogs with many experiences. Just below our kennels is a small field with sheep, chickens and other livestock in it. Every day the dogs run through the animals on the way to exercise and they quickly learn steadiness in this way. The odd accident happens, of course, but punishment is swift and instant and the young dog tends not to make

Dogs appreciate a cooling swim in hot weather

the same mistake twice. Here again, with a little imagination, the one-dog person can show the dog pet rabbits, take him to fields with stock in them, or walk him round the hen run. Of course he should be kept on a lead until you are 100 per cent certain of his steadiness for farmers do not take kindly to folk training dogs at the expense of a flock of breeding ewes. Failing that, many trainers have rabbit pens for this purpose, and would be amenable to being asked if you could try your dog in them.

Feeding

We provide tripe twice a day, a handful of dry biscuits scattered in each run in the morning and a full meal later in the day. It does not matter at what time you give the main meal but it is important that it is at the same time every day so that the dog develops a routine. This should not vary and the more strictly you can stick to the same times of doing things with your dog, the better. Like many humans, dogs like to know where they stand.

I have no strong views about what proprietory brands to feed. If the dog looks well on what you are giving him and seems to like it, then there is no point in changing. I have used them all from tinned dog meat mixed with biscuit to the all-in-one foods and find that they all have their strengths and weaknesses. When I have whelping bitches for which only the very best will do, I do admit a preference for the American Febo food, sometimes called Purina. This is too expensive to feed on a regular basis but if I had to stick my neck out and choose one food, it would be that. Basically, though, find one that is readily available, that the dog likes and on which the dog looks well and you will be about right.

Kitchen scraps should also be used, strained vegetable water and bits and pieces are all full of valuable nutrients and should not be wasted. They help add a little interest to what can otherwise become a boring and repetitive diet. Eggs are fine in spite of recent scares, but use the yolks only for the whites can cause constipation. As for bones – another vexing issue – if you have only one dog raw beef bones are acceptable. We give no bones here for all our dogs are kennelled in twos and bones invariably lead to fighting, even if you give the dogs one each. A good raw leg bone of a steer (not cooked on any account) will keep a dog busy for hours, exercise his jaws and neck muscles, keep him out of mischief and prevent him growing bored. On no account ever let a dog eat the bones of birds such as chickens or pheasants. They can splinter to needle-sharp points and penetrate a dog's gut in extreme cases and lead to all sorts of problems.

Dog feeding has changed greatly since I was a lad. When I was fifteen years old I was given the job of preparing the dog food. I made ready a huge cauldron full of boiling water. The head keeper came along at the critical moment and threw in a handful of salt. Then I took the 'fallen' animals, dead sheep and cows, casualties which we had collected and cut them up and dropped them into the water. These were well boiled and at the end, the head keeper returned and tossed fishmeal, a quantity of oatmeal and a pinch of his own, secret, magic ingredient into the pot. It was critical that this was added in just the right amount. When it was cool it went solid and could be carved with a long knife into rich, meat-packed chunks, loaded with all the extras needed for a full diet and the dogs looked excellent on it. Sadly such a method is rather too labour intensive for today.

The ideal test of good feeding is to inspect your dog's droppings. They should be firm and not runny. Also, if a dog is being properly fed, he should not need to move his bowels more than once a day. This is one of the most reliable home checks you can carry out on the general state of a dog's immediate health.

Grooming and General Care

I do not bother much with grooming unless a dog has got himself into an especially bad mess. Spaniels and burrs can be a problem but we clip their ears to make cleaning them easier after a hard day in the field. I do go to a bit of trouble if Her Majesty the Queen is coming down so that the dogs look their best for her, but generally speaking, dogs are very good at mutual grooming. As I explained, our dogs are kennelled in twos and often after a shooting day they will come home filthy and wet. If I take the trouble to peep in at them, they are busy cleaning each other and in a surprisingly short time, they are as spotless as if they had never been out.

As for drying wet dogs, this is another contentious issue. My father was a great gundog man and he held the view that rubbing the coat with a towel, chamois leather, newspaper or whatever else is not recommended. It only rubs the moisture into the dog's fur and does not absorb it properly. The wood wool and heat lamp combination we use here is perfect and we do not rub down the dogs at all. The worst thing possible you can do is to take a dripping wet dog home and allow him to curl up in front of a roaring fire and go to sleep. This can be fatal in the long term and leads to all sorts of aches and pains. For the one-dog owner, allow the dog to dry off naturally in a warm, but not hot, place rather than rubbing all the wet into his insulating layer of under fur and making him really wet. The strong, bright guard hairs on a labrador's coat are water repellent anyway. Search deep among them for the skin and even on the wettest day you will find the dog quite dry underneath.

It is important that a cold, wet and exhausted dog should be given a snack immediately after work. I hear of cases (our distinguished editor being one) who have had utterly reliable dogs which, left in cars after a long day, have chewed at anything which takes their fancy, from waxproof coats to shot game and the handles of picnic baskets. This is only the dog trying to take in some nourishment to build up his body heat and combat the tiredness and cold. Either have a wire dog cage in the back of your vehicle or give the dog a handful of biscuits or, better still, both.

All our dogs live to a good old age with fourteen or fifteen being common. I recently had a dog of sixteen which is a great age for a working labrador. Rheumatism is rare among them and so I feel that my wet-dog theory is correct, if only because of the results we see in our own kennels. Many a man who religiously rubs his dog after a fowling trip and dries him off by the fire is likely to encounter more problems than we, who simply leave the dogs to clean themselves and dry off gradually in a draught-free environment.

Ear mites are a regular problem. They originate in cats and dogs will pick them up easily. Oddly enough the mites do not trouble cats but they are a nuisance to dogs. The middle ear is irritated so that the dog regularly and violently shakes his head with the eventual result that the tips of his ears develop sores which take a long time to heal. There are several treatments available from the vet for this trouble and we treat the dogs every two weeks for it with a preparation called GAC. Regular treatment is best and preferable to waiting for a severe infection before taking action. What is more, the dog grows used to having the medicine squirted into his ear so that the matter becomes routine. A dog unfamiliar with the treatment puts up stern resistance.

Worms can be another problem and they need regular dosing. We use Shaw's Earlyworm, but there are several effective medications available and your vet will advise you; it is always wise to follow his instructions, no matter how much you think you know. We treat puppies at 3, 5 and again at 7 weeks. Mature dogs are treated once every twelve months. A sudden build-up can be detected by the dog's coat growing dry and listless, a greatly increased appetite and, in advanced cases, signs of fragments of worm in the motions. In such cases a single course of treatment will usually cure the infestation. Fleas similarly are treated regularly with powder, for the life cycle of the flea is related to that of the intestinal worm and one should not treat one without treating the other.

Dogs which suffer from acute stiffness after hard work can be treated with 'Bute' available from the vet and more usually used on horses. I have had no practical experience of this but have heard that it can be effective. Although we shoot here quite often, we have a large enough squad of dogs to prevent any single one becoming over-tired and exhausted.

In common with almost every other working dog trainer and breeder, we always remove the dew claws. They may be taken off quickly and virtually painlessly five days after birth and then you are free forever of a potential problem. Dew claws in adult life catch on barbed wire, tear on rough heather and are a liability. They have no practical use to the dog and are leftovers from the ancient days when dogs walked on all five toes. We also dock the tails of spaniels, again an almost universal practice but there are some changes recommended by the EEC which might well result in this becoming outlawed throughout the European Community. I view this as a bad step; the thought of a long-tailed spaniel working in the rough cover and brambles we have here and which you will find on many shoots where spaniels are used, fills me with alarm. I can only hope that good sense prevails and that this unwise piece of legislation does not become law.

There comes a sad time in the life of every dog-owner, probably more than once in his lifetime, when his dog comes to the end of his working life. He will have spent a period of honourable retirement and the time comes when, due to physical infirmities, he has to be put down. This is a nettle which must be grasped firmly. To prolong needlessly the life of a dog which has become a burden and an embarrassment to himself is selfish and cruel. This is no way to treat an old and faithful servant for all his years of loyalty and hard work. There are those who go the whole way and shoot the dog themselves. I do not recommend this and feel that anyone who can do that is not really at heart a dog-lover. It does not bear thinking about that something might go wrong or your shot be ill-placed. I could not even consider doing such a thing. Equally important is that you see the job through yourself by taking the dog to the vet. Do not delegate this to someone else for to do so is to shirk your own responsibility. You have a duty to the dog to be there at the end, to reassure him in strange surroundings and to be present when he needs you most. Modern veterinary science has evolved substances which are painless with no stress attached to their administration. The dog simply grows drowsy and falls into his last, long sleep. *Your* arm should be around him at that moment, not that of a stranger. Such is one of the less palatable responsibilities of dog-ownership.

Our pensioners are retired gracefully. Sidney was thirteen when he was withdrawn from active service. He was a great and famous dog, whose picture looks down on me from the wall every day. He spent his last two years living in the house. I took him out to help with training the young dogs where he would sit patiently waiting for a go and I always tried to give him a retrieve at the end and he would proudly carry the dummy home with me and up the garden path. One of his finest hours was at the last Stratfield Saye Game Fair. He was a great performer and responded well to a crowd, better there, in fact, than he was in the field. Many gundog people still speak to me about his showing on that day. Along with our other old faithful friends and servants, he lies buried in the special dog cemetery on the estate.

Travelling can prove a problem unless you are careful. Many complain that their dogs are car sick and make a fearful mess in the vehicle every time they are taken out. I must say, I am not all that surprised as the way I see many people drive these days would make me car sick, let alone a dog! It

might be considered unreasonable to put a new dog in a modern car, drive a hundred miles to go shooting and expect him to behave perfectly. Many a child would not be able to manage such an ordeal. The trick is to allow the dog gradually to become accustomed to the car and the place within it he is expected to occupy. We have an old estate car here which we use for that purpose. The dogs grow used to jumping in and out of it (only on command) and sometimes I give them a biscuit or two when they are in it so that they have only good associations with the car and learn that there is nothing to fear. When you are driving to and from your shooting, try to remember that you have a dog on board and take extra care on the corners and with sudden braking.

The usual family estate car is quite good enough for transporting dogs. The important things are that there should be room for a good circulation of air, room for the dog to lie down at full length and a suitable base material such as sacking, Drybed, newspaper, or something which can be easily removed and cleaned when the car is required for family business. Some dogs become possessive about their cars and will allow no other dog near, let alone share it as a fellow traveller. Again commonsense and a little planning can overcome this problem. Allow the strange dog into the car first and only then put in the usual occupant who will more readily accept the stranger if he is already *in situ.* Alternatively, allow both dogs to run around and play together so that by the time you need to put them in the car they have grown accustomed to each other. The modern shooting man is very mobile, used to travelling many hundreds of miles in a season for his sport. A dog that will not travel would prove a very severe handicap.

When we travel up to Balmoral which we do every year for the grouse

Accustom your dog to vehicles from an early age

Special dog-carrying trailer – expensive, but it spares the upholstery

shooting, we take twenty-eight dogs in a special, 2 ton van, equipped with food, feeding equipment and everything we or they are likely to need. Oddly enough, we noticed that even with our careful vehicle training, the long journey caused the dogs to lose condition far more quickly than any amount of hard work in the field.

The special compartments which you can buy for the backs of estate cars or vans are very useful. The best are light and airy, may be easily taken in or out of the vehicle, and have the effect of keeping all the mud and hairs away from the upholstery. A wet dog in a car is bound to spread his presence and this might not go down well with other members of the family. The special car kennels are available in sizes to suit almost any vehicle and to take one or more dogs of various sizes, with or without a separating compartment.

There should be no room in any kennel, no matter how large or small, for a fighter or a biter. There is an old saying that to have a fighting dog you must be a fighting man and unless you are the world heavyweight champion, you will have a miserable shooting life if your dog cannot be trusted not to start a brawl when he is not directly under your eye – and sometimes even when he is. Can you imagine us taking our twenty-eight dogs to Scotland on a journey which lasts a good ten hours and having a fighter among them? A fighting dog causes trouble on a shooting day, makes the owner unpopular and is likely to cost him a few invitations if he refuses to take the hints which his fellow guns will not be slow to drop in his direction. Not only that, but the sport of the owner is ruined if he cannot relax for a moment to enjoy a chat or a bite of lunch because he is worried about whom or what his dog is about to savage next. The best gundog in the world is no good to me if he is a fighter. Damage might be caused to the dogs of other guests, in short the whole thing is a miserable experience and should not be tolerated. Such a dog should be given away to a home where no other dogs are likely to be encountered, or to a lone pigeon- or roughshooter where he can do no damage.

However, dogs are territorial animals and also they tend to establish a pecking order of seniority among themselves and this should be respected. The best behaved dog will defend his kennel, his food and other things he considers important to him and the wise owner sees to it that he does not trespass on this or allow or even encourage other dogs to do the same. As in many gundog-training matters, anticipation and a basic knowledge of canine psychology will solve many problems before they occur.

Punishment is another problem which no doubt some of the other contributors to this book will cover. My own view is that a good shaking with the dog's front legs off the ground is best. This must be administered at the time when the dog is caught in the act of the crime. It is no good calling the dog back to you and then punishing him, for he cannot then associate the crime with the punishment. When one of our dogs catches a chicken in the field, I chase it and try and catch him with the chicken still in his mouth. In that way, the dog knows precisely why he is being rebuked.

Make full use of your vet; find a good one and stick to him or her, for you are paying them to help you. It is a mistake to undertake home treatment unless you know precisely what you are doing. I have learned to remove surgical stitches for dogs are occasionally cut on wire or some other obstruction, and I can squeeze clear the anal glands, both easy enough jobs

when you know how and for the regular dog person, well worth learning.

Barking at night can be a nuisance if you live surrounded by neighbours. This happens for no particular reason. In our case it might be because one dog will not allow the other into the bed, because the dog is bored, has heard strange and unfamiliar noises or is too full of energy and underexercised. The old psychology as discovered by Pavlov comes into play again. Shout 'Quiet!', run down in your dressing gown and administer punishment. You should have to do this no more than twice, often once will do. If the barking is repeated you have only to shout 'Quiet!' out of the window, the dog will guess what is likely to happen next and grow suddenly silent.

If you have to go away or on holiday and are unable to take the dogs it is best, if you can, to leave them at home. They are on familiar ground and will be happiest there, but you must have someone utterly reliable whom the dogs know, to feed and exercise them. If you are let down in this way it is disastrous. If no such person is available, go for boarding kennels but be sure to pick a good one. Some are less than satisfactory, so you owe it to yourself and to the dogs to carry out a preliminary visit to make sure your dogs will be well looked after. Many kennels are very good indeed and dogs come back wormed, de-fleaed and sometimes in better shape then when they went away!

Many members of the Royal Family are keen and expert gundog trainers and handlers. Many of their dogs are here in the kennels now. Her Majesty the Queen is especially keen and the dogs always know when she has arrived to see them. I am a great believer that dogs have a sixth sense denied us humans, for long before I know it, the Queen's own dogs will leave my side and run to her and completely ignore me for the rest of the day. She has an amazing mutual understanding with her dogs which are devoted to her. The secret is that she builds up a good relationship with them and sees them quite often. If more handlers had that one knack, there would be a good many better dogs about.

With one or other of the dogs Her Majesty has carried out many a spectacular retrieve. I recall one on the grouse moor, when a bird towered and fell a good 800yd away, over a valley, across a little burn and on a peat hag on top of the next hill. The black labrador bitch named Sherry, a real beauty and a wonderful animal, had not marked it, but Her Majesty sent her, got her across the river and up the hill and even onto the plateau which involved a jump of some feet. Then a grouse flushed and flew off, but it was a different bird. The bitch had left the peat hag, but Her Majesty got her up back again and eventually the bird was picked. The whole thing took a good quarter of an hour. By then all the guns, beaters and pickers-up had assembled for a grandstand view and everybody clapped when, at last, the bird was delivered to hand. The Princess Royal is probably one of the best pickers-up we have at Sandringham with a rare touch with dogs and a persistence on a runner which fills the bag many times.

A healthy, happy dog is top on your list of priorities

I do not do much shooting myself and am not all that keen. I have done more than my share in my time but working and training the dogs is a far more satisfying way to me of spending a shooting day. There is always something new to be seen and done while just pulling the trigger can lose its novelty if you have done it often enough. Years ago when I lived in Fife I went out shooting on New Year's Day. Not a soul was to be seen for they were all recovering from hogmanay the night before. My friend and I spent the morning ferreting on a crisp frosty day with bright sun. The rabbits bolted well. We walked about 4 miles accompanied by a rough labrador and a terrier and must have bagged about forty rabbits. My friend took the bag home on his bicycle and I walked home. On the way I flushed two cock pheasants and shot them both. A little further on I came upon a stubble with duck flighting in to feed. I had only ten cartridges left. These I fired and shot four mallard. It was a perfect day, and one which will always stay in my memory. I think that more shooting ought to be of that nature instead of the desire for bigger and bigger bags of reared pheasants which you could hit with a frying pan.

Dogs remain the lasting pleasure for me in shooting and I end where I began. Look after your dog and he will look after you and give you years of companionship and hard work and you will derive endless pleasure from each other's company. Learn to watch your dog. You will be able to tell from his demeanour, the state of his coat, the brightness of his eye, how he plays, how he barks, how he carries his tail, the state of his motions and many other things how he is faring. You are both an element of a partnership. You must see to it that you keep your part of the bargain by offering the best care and attention to your dog's comforts that you are able.

Drake

JOHN HUMPHREYS

Built in similar mould but of a completely different temperament to Cassius was Drake, one of the best working dogs I have been lucky enough to own. Again, very little credit is due to me, for he picked it up on his own account and knew rather more about the ways of game and wildfowl than many humans I could mention. I got him thanks to a tip from Chris Hopwood, that all-round dog and shooting gamekeeper who put me onto Angus Nudds, noted keeper of Bedfordshire who just happened to have a litter of likely pups at the moment I was recovering from the trauma of Cassius. In later life Angus was to remind me of the transaction and, in view of how well Drake was to turn out, would not let me forget that, 'You had him too cheap'.

I cannot think why it should be but Drake was another in the run of large, raw-boned, independent dogs which seemed to find their way into my kennels. He was pleasant and biddable, a mite headstrong when working but he knew that he, and not I, was the expert and acted accordingly. Of all my dogs he was with me longest, went out with me most often and shared more experiences in the field with me than any other. He retrieved my first grouse; he had such a love of water and contempt for ice and cold that he ferried duck after duck over the mat of rotting weed and back to me, and he earned the name and reputation as a bag-filler.

He was full of work and it was hard to make him stop. During a break for lunch he would be snuffling round the farm buildings, sneaking off when my back was turned, doing a little hunting on his own account. He was a dog for all seasons, though, and did not mind waiting at a peg; his chameleon-like character making him the perfect all-round dog for every shooting occasion.

He died quite young, but he just wore himself out and at ten he was done, battle scarred, gaunt, great muscles grown flaccid, grizzled head laid low. I sat out in a deck-chair one fateful time, not under the broiling sun of that hot mid-June but in the ghostly pallor of a midsummer moon. The air was heavy and humid, the scent of

'*A young dog may find himself up against all sorts of difficult places in the shooting field . . .*'

Well trained dogs sit steadily where they are dropped, whatever their masters might be doing

(Opposite) *Spaniels are ideal dogs for rough country*

(Overleaf) *Sturdy puppies, and plenty of room for everyone*

the honeysuckle which drooped thickly over the door was so strong as to be overpow-
ering. Midnight tolled from the church tower across the meadow, an owl hooted,
a cock pheasant called twice, sharply, as something suspicious scuttled beneath his
roosting tree. Moths blundered among the blossoms and I was there with my pipe
and my thoughts; tomorrow was the start of the coarse-fishing season.

But I was thinking not of fishing but of dogs; not of any dog but of the dog which
lay at my feet. Like a Hollywood B picture a succession of flashbacks flickered across
the mind's eye as the high and low spots of a decade came cleanly and crisply back.
The moon slid from behind a thin cloud and bathed the lawn in a coppery glow. It
was a similar moon but one in January five years before which shone more coldly
on the saltings: the dog and I shivered in a creek, for the spartina was rimed with
ice and the dry rustle of the tide 2 miles away sounded close enough to make me
anxious. The wigeon awoke with the moon and began to move. Flickering wings
and silver whistling came from all sides and small parties began to swirl round
and drop into the flash over which Drake and I crouched – dangerous sentinels.

A full moon with little cloud made for hard shooting, but then some filmy whisps
drifted over to give a modest covering and the birds might now be seen. It was not
such difficult shooting, for my first two shots knocked down a brace then I got two
with one barrel, missed the next three, made an effort and dropped the following
three until I had eleven birds down. The cloud was thickening and there was a lull
so Drake began to pick up and collected every single one. Then there was snow on
the breeze, big, fat flakes of it plopping onto my shoulders and, in seconds, a once
black labrador was two toned with a wide shelf of snow from his ears to the root
of his tail but, by contrast looking all the blacker underneath. Every point of his
hair held a drop of ice and he was hard and prickly to the touch. The flight was
as good as over, but in a final flurry I shot six more, all of which he recovered and
we marched off triumphantly with seventeen birds picked and not one lost.

The next recollection took us hundreds of miles north to the moor where we
plodded upwards and onwards through the bee-buzzing August heather. A grouse
rose in front, was hard hit but towered, flew in an enormous circle back across one
valley and almost on to the next before it collapsed and fell. No dog but one would
go half that distance but Drake had marked it and he set off like a greyhound from
the trap, scorning the easy route, straight across peat hags and mountain becks until
he was a black dot in the purple haze. He found the bird immediately and came
galloping back to a patter of applause from the gallery and an owner who flushed
with pride and basked in the reflected glory of his performance.

Less happy but equally characteristic was the January cock shoot in his more
mature years when we were sent to blank in the fir planting and hedge which surrounded it. It was very strictly a cocks-only day at the fag end of the season but the
dog pegged and brought to hand a succession of no less than six hen pheasants and
an enormous Moran chicken. He was getting slightly hard mouthed by this time and
while none of these birds showed visible signs of injury, they seemed unable to either
stand up or fly but keeled over and died in a most distressing manner. I was obliged

to proffer the keeper this monstrous bag with the best excuses I could muster.

Next, my mental computer clicked back seven years to a windy night by a Scottish sea loch. The eight bore had spoken to good effect and a single greylag had turned on its back, half recovered and tumbled down to splash in an explosion of white spray. One wing stuck up like a dying salute but the offshore breeze caught this impromptu sail and drifted the bird out steadily onto the mile of tumbled grey water dotted with sheets of drifting ice which lay ahead. The dog set out on a gruelling swim and was a good 300yd offshore by the time he made the pick-up. He turned to come back but now the wind and waves were in his face and that great wing was still catching the breeze. At times he seemed hardly to move, at others the distant speck vanished altogether while I ran dementedly up and down the shoreline, urging, whistling and encouraging. Like Horatius wounded and in full armour swimming the Tiber, his chin was borne bravely up and after what seemed an agonising age of waiting he was in the shallows. He delivered the bird, vomited a pail of seawater and collapsed on the sand where he lay under my coat for fully quarter of an hour before recovering.

Back even further in time we were down on a friendly little freshwater marsh by a fen river where once I had the shooting. Its problem was a treacherous raft of rotting reed, the accumulated rubbish of decades, which bordered the wide, meandering river. There was a steep, thistle-clad bank on the far side. The prevailing wind and the flightlines tended to take birds over the river, while any which had even a spark of life still in them, often struggled as far as that bank before collapsing, often falling out of sight beyond it. A dog retrieving had to negotiate the quaking, floating bog, swim the river and work on or over the jungle on the far bank. It was a good place but one or two special nights stick in the mind such as when a friend and I killed thirty-two teal in a gale in an hour and a half. The general picture, backed up by statistics from the game book, shows a great many duck killed in Drake's lifetime at this place, most of them retrieved by him and no more than a score or so lost. Time after time he crossed that river and heaved himself back but seldom let me down, doing his best to please even when I asked the unreasonable of him and sent him more often than I should.

For a labrador he was a good all-rounder, knowing how to behave on a driven day, although he did once course and kill a wounded hare in front of the guest of honour when we were picking up on a posh shoot. He enjoyed a rough day and learned the knack of working the choked fen dykes, prancing from side to side, leaping fences, bustling and thrashing out the pheasants which had tucked themselves snugly in the thickest places, but rarely forgetting himself and working too far ahead. Many a time he filled the bag for me and took it as a personal insult if we came home empty-handed. He would peg a bird if I had failed to shoot one, once bringing me someone else's four-pricked wigeon on our walk back from a blank morning flight. It was Gill Richards who gave him the name 'The Bag-filling Dog' on the day when he stole a grouse from under the nose of her puppy – I was powerless to stop him, it was pure instinct – and the nickname stuck. He could roustabout one day for rough-lying pheasants, lurk in the pigeon hide, crouch with me for geese, ride in the punt or sit calmly at a peg on a partridge shoot as though butter would not melt . . .

As a character he was placid, dignified and gentle, fond of children and loved a game of rough and tumble. Life sat easily upon him and he kept his enormous energy and extrovert deeds to the shooting field. He was a large, craggy dog with a slightly Roman nose and very pale brown eyes; I recall him well and his photograph looks down on me as I write. In his last season he was doing half days and gloriously wiping the eyes of younger dogs by flushing and retrieving birds which they had missed.

Now he lay at my feet, that great heart quite worn out and failing by the hour, that seemingly inexhaustible energy spent, able only to give a single thresh of his tail when I touched him. He had done so much for me without complaint for so many years, we had enjoyed some remarkable adventures together, travelled thousands of miles and made many human and canine friends in that time. If I make to leave my deck-chair and go to bed, he whines feebly; the least I can do is keep him company on this, the last one of many vigils we have kept together.

In the early morning as the moon set, painlessly and without a fuss Drake died. I buried him on the marsh beneath the old willow tree, scene of many of his shooting adventures so that he might see the duck coming in on autumn evenings. As the Spaniards say, 'May the earth lie light upon him'.

Picking-up

ROBIN WISE

Robin Wise spent many years watching her husband trialling labradors before acquiring her first gundog twelve years ago after a series of injuries had ended her competitive activities on horses. Her first dog proved too hot for trialling but excellent at picking-up. Next she bought another puppy which was very successful at field trials. Since then her doggy interests have been equally divided between trialling and picking-up. She has trialled several other dogs with varying degrees of success and is currently field trial secretary of the East Anglian Labrador Retriever Club. She now trains labradors for other people as well as for herself. She has a knowledge of shoot management as her husband runs a shoot. She is therefore able to assess the role of picking-up from a viewpoint other than that of a specialist dog-handler. She picks up regularly on several shoots and is often out four days a week. This involves a sympathetic back-up from home as supper and other housewifely duties can get neglected.

Every shoot, however small, needs pickers-up. The number of people required to do this varies from shoot to shoot. I think that it is almost impossible for one person to cover a line of eight guns so the minimum number should be two. They justify their existence if they pick-up one wounded bird in a day which would not otherwise have been found. This job is done by people up and down the country who have one thing in common – they enjoy working their dogs. Every breed of gundog is used and, although I have a personal preference for labradors, I would never decry any other breed. The important thing is to have good dogs, keen but trustworthy, and then every day's picking-up is enjoyable. It is a satisfying and useful occupation. It certainly keeps you fit and enables you to meet all sorts of interesting people.

The writer after a successful foray

I have been picking-up for about ten years. I am usually out three or four days a week, attending four shoots regularly with a few extra days here and there. I can only write this chapter from my own experience. Pickers-up find themselves in all sorts of circumstances from walking a hedgerow with one or two guns to picking-up on large commercial shoots. The hedgerow situation has, in my case, often involved my children and their friends when they were learning to shoot. One experienced dog was taken on these expeditions, essentially one which was a specialist at finding difficult runners.

The other end of the picking-up spectrum is the commercial shoot. At such shoots, it is best to have several dogs and expect to pick-up large numbers of birds during the day. Sometimes the guns will have no dogs of their own, if, for example, they have come from abroad. The picking-up team will then need to do all the work and, if the guns have taken five hundred plus birds, that is going to involve a lot of work for pickers-up. A good team is vital so that birds are not wasted or left wounded. Some of the time the dogs will be acting as 'hoovers', clearing up behind the guns. Good hunting dogs, however, are important so that runners which might have tucked themselves into the undergrowth or, alternatively, gone great distances, are all picked up. When guns are paying large amounts of money for a day, they are entitled to expect that all aspects of the shoot are run efficiently and enthusiastically. I have heard guns say that they had taken a day on such and such a famous shoot but had not enjoyed it because, over the years, the standards had slipped. The reason seemed to be that the regular team of beaters and pickers-up were treating it as just another day, a boring job which had to be done. The initial enthusiastic atmosphere had gone from the shoot and the guns were treated as just another team. This is an unforgiveable attitude.

The picking-up which I do all through the shooting season is on private shoots where between seventy and two hundred and fifty birds are shot. I feel that I can get real job satisfaction on that size of shoot as I can usually see the hit birds and have time to watch where they go and the opportunity to go and find them. The shoots are varied. One is mainly partridges, the others pheasants. One is a syndicate, the others not. One is all in thick cover, one is nearly all in the open and the others are mixed. I enjoy them equally and they provide a great variety of work for experienced dogs and opportunities to start young ones.

I now want to describe what the hosts and keepers expect of the pickers-up. I will follow this with the attitudes of the guns towards us, and finally try to explain my own approach to the job. I want to do this because I think it is all very relevant to anyone who is thinking of starting picking-up. In one of my other capacities, as a field trial secretary, I see some new people each year coming into the sport who must be doing some picking-up somewhere – they should not be trialling if they are not. Occasional ones seem to have very little idea of game sense, of whether a bird is going to run or not, of how to use wind direction to the dog's advantage or even of understanding what their own dogs are doing. A lot of people come to the sport through training classes and working tests. These may have an important function in teaching people to train dogs up to a point but there is so much more to learn and it takes a lifetime to learn it all. Some people forget this.

Hosts and Keepers

The host and the keeper view the pickers-up in much the same way. It is important not to forget that they have asked you there and, if you want to continue, you must do everything you can to do a good job for them. They want the picker-up to collect all the wounded game with as little disturbance to the rest of the shoot as possible. I stress *all* the wounded game because it is no good taking just your young dog to a shoot and then saying that you are sorry but that you cannot pick that wounded hare or that runner disappearing over the skyline because it would ruin your dog. I find it essential to have an older dog or two which I don't worry too much about sending for everything. I can then pick and choose the retrieves that I want for my young dog. I ruined my first dog's steadiness for trialling by sending her for everything when she was very young. I did not want to let the host down and get the sack as a result. This particular bitch never ceased to be brilliant at picking-up, probably the best I have ever had, but as she grew older, I did have to put her on a lead during drives.

The other thing that matters to the host is that dogs of pickers-up are under control and in no danger of going off and ruining the next drive. To me, picking-up is no fun at all if I have taken a dog that I am worried about and feel that I could blow my whistle with no response at all. For example, on one famous small shoot where I pick-up belonging to Will Garfit, the artist, the whole area is only 70 acres of thick cover and water. The bag is nearly always around one hundred head. All the drives are very close together and the cover is so thick that your dog is out of sight as soon as you have sent him. It is vital, on this shoot, to have complete trust in your dog and know that when you blow your whistle he will pay attention and come back to you, otherwise you would spend the whole day in serious danger of ruining not only the next drive but every other drive of the day. Will used to give me an

The writer picks a bird from thick cover – that is her job

The picker-up should be well behind the line of guns

illustrated map of the shoot to make sure I understood where not to let the dogs go. It is vitally important to the host and the keeper that the pickers-up are well briefed in the plan for the day. I once got lost on a fen shoot, through my own stupid fault, and I walked miles to where I heard shooting, only to discover when I got there that I had walked into a neighbouring shoot. The poor host had to send out a search party to find me.

I am happiest if I have my own transport so that I can spend time looking for birds after the guns have gone to the next drive. It can be very frustrating to be travelling with the guns or beaters and not have time to look for the long-distance runner for fear of holding up the whole shoot. The host and keeper are often very tense on a shoot day and the last thing they want is for all the guns to be delayed because the picker-up is missing. When birds are lost and there is no time to look for them it is important to tell the keeper so that he can look the next day.

Anybody who goes to a new shoot will inevitably not do a brilliant job on his first day there. He should spend that day learning how the shoot works and where the birds fly. He should not try to impress everyone there that his dogs are better than any they have seen before. Rather, he should go exactly where he is told and pick-up whatever he can while being absolutely certain that he is not straying on to forbidden territory. First impressions are important. One keeper thought I was useless for a long time because I never carry a game bag. He was not to know that I have one weak shoulder which aches if I carry anything over it. I prefer a game carrier which can go in my pocket until I have a lot of birds to carry. In summary, the host and keeper expect the picker-up to bring back all the wounded game, to keep his dogs under control and to attempt to be in the right place at the right time.

Attitude of the Guns

My husband said to me, when I first started picking-up, that if I got shot it would be my own fault. He was quite right and it was a very important lesson. Guns hate to be inhibited in their shooting by thinking that the picker-up is too close, and so no picker-up, therefore, should be closer than 250yd. There is no point in being close, you are not there to pick-up dead birds round the pegs. Provided you are far enough away you can send the dog for runners quickly during the drive and have a far greater chance of picking them. You must make sure that nobody minds if you do this. Occasionally there are specific instructions not to pick-up until the drive is over.

Guns often have their own dogs and they get a great deal of pleasure in working them after the drive. A picker-up, in my opinion, should never, under any circumstances, send a dog to any dead bird shot by a gun with his own dog unless specifically asked to do so. Time and again I have seen pickers-up, field triallers are often the worst offenders, showing off that they can handle their dogs at long distances, by sending them towards the guns for dead birds that the latter may well want to pick-up themselves. If the picker-up is in a position to do this, he is almost certainly too close. A friend of mine with a good dog of his own took an expensive day in Wales recently. His enjoyment was ruined because the dogs of the pickers-up were totally out of control, running-in, picking-up birds around him and his dog, changing birds and then returning to their handlers. After each drive he simply did not know which birds had been picked and he could seldom send his own dog for anything.

There are occasions when the pickers-up cannot get far enough away from the guns because there is a river or a motorway or some other obstacle in the way. If this happens, the safest answer is for the picker-up to stand in the line with a gun. If, however, the host specifically asks him to go to a certain place and this is within range of the guns, it is extremely important that he makes certain that they know where he is. The most foolhardy thing that he can do is to squat down and try to hide from them. They will get as much of a fright as the picker-up will if they are suddenly looking at him down gun barrels.

Guns often hit birds without knowing it. I have proved this when standing with my husband. He has on more than one occasion told me I was mad to go and look for a bird which I knew he had hit. He has been surprised when I have returned with that bird. It is important to try to tell the guns if you pick birds that they are unaware of having touched. There are two reasons for this. One is that they will be delighted. The other reason is that they will more readily believe that the bag total at the end of the day has not been increased with pegged birds.

I like guns who show an interest in whether their birds are picked or not. I have known some to wander off to the next drive, not seeming to care about their wounded birds. These are, thank goodness, very much in the minority. Most will take the trouble to find the picker-up if they are in any doubt that he has not seen any of their wounded birds. Alternatively, they will tell the keeper who can pass the message on. Caring guns will often ask me several drives later whether I have picked certain birds which they shot on a previous drive. Some, I am sure, go home thinking that the picker-up is useless if he has not found every single bird that he has looked for during the day. It is, however, unlikely that he will find everything, and he can only do his best.

Guns can be very helpful to the picker-up if they can mark down their own birds. When a big flush occurs it is impossible for the picker-up

Some guns prefer to retrieve their own birds if they are dead and lying nearby. The picker-up should be elsewhere

Pickers-up wait in the places wounded birds are likely to find

to watch everything simultaneously. Some guns are very accurate markers and you get to know who to trust as you set off across two large fields to look for a bird down by a certain oak tree on the skyline. Others, however, are not so precise and pickers-up will always have tales to tell about certain guns who have endlessly sent them great distances for birds that are never found. 'I hit a bird hard that went 300yd in that direction,' they say with conviction. Did they hit them, was it wishful thinking or did they just give you a mark that was completely wrong? The picker-up should always try for these birds. He should never dismiss them as a probable fairy tale. This can be a temptation especially at the end of the day when he and his dogs are tired.

Guns also seem to have a problem with counting up to more than about three! They are, occasionally, prepared to admit that they get in a muddle after a big drive. Sometimes, however, they will state with conviction that they have picked everything around them. However, I will always, if time permits, hunt the dogs around their pegs after they have gone. Rarely do I fail to find one that they have forgotten about.

In summary, guns do not want the picker-up too close to them. They want to work their own dogs whenever they can. They want all their runners picked, if possible, and they are always grateful for all that is found for them.

Approach to the Job

Now I come on to describe the job from my own vantage point. As I have already stated, my picking-up is varied. I start on a partridge shoot in October by which time I have got my dogs fit. The weather is often dry and warm. Many partridges fall on open plough and these can be surprisingly difficult for the dogs to find. There is often no scent and slow, careful dogs are more successful than those which race about.

The busy months are November and December when all 'my shoots' are in full swing. The bags are larger so the dogs are working hard. In the Christmas holidays I am involved in many boys' days which often produce the most challenging picking-up. Finally, in January, there are helpers' days and cocks-only days. At this time, there is often snow or heavy ground-frost. These conditions, again, make for very little scent.

As in every other sport, there are good days and bad ones. Bad scenting days can be very frustrating. I have, many times, been near to tears when the dogs don't seem to be able to find anything. On these days I can be quite convinced that the guns think that my dogs are useless and I begin to think the same. I go home feeling thoroughly miserable. The worst thing that can happen on that sort of day is to get 'eye-wiped' by one of the gun's dogs. If my dogs have been searching for a bird for ten minutes and a gun strolls along and picks it with his dog, I can feel like giving up altogether. Luckily, however, these sorts of days are few and far between. More often, you go home at the end of the day feeling that your dogs have done a good job and that most of the birds have been picked.

Just as a gun remembers certain high pheasants that he has shot, so a picker-up remembers specific retrieves. There are days when everything seems to go right and every bird is found. These are the days I remember best. I recall standing with a gun beside the River Cam with my old dog, Quiver. The gun shot nine pheasants into some very thick rough over the river, several of which were not dead. She swam the river nine times and found and brought back every one. I remember finding a woodcock for Archie Coates, the famous pigeon shooter, which every other dog at Will Garfit's shoot that day had tried and failed to find. I remember several guns watching Tremble take a runner round two sides of one field, across another and finally find it in the ditch beyond. 'It won't have gone far,' the gun had said. All pickers-up will remember these sorts of retrieves. If they are trialling people, they will wish they had occurred during a trial because it is such retrieves that win stakes.

A Good Dog

I am lucky enough to have several dogs and, just as there are 'horses for courses' so there are certain dogs which are better than others in different circumstances. They are all different and have different qualities.

Some mark well. If I know I am going to be picking-up in roots, I will try to take a good marking dog that I can rely on to go straight to the fall of a wounded bird. The dog which is at the fall quickly is so much more likely to pick the bird than the one which has to be handled to the right spot by which time the bird is half a field away. If I know I am going to be picking-up in thick woodland, marking is not so important but a dog which will hunt and persevere all day is what is required. Certain experienced dogs will learn the knack of knowing the line and distance to go into a wood for hit birds even when the trees prevent them from getting accurate marks. Some dogs, I am sure, develop an almost uncanny sense of knowing when a bird is hit even when it is still in the air. Of course, they are not always right and one must be careful that these dogs do not make their own decisions when they think their stupid masters are not paying attention.

Dogs have different systems of hunting out a wood after a drive. There are those which cover large areas and act as good hoovers while others hunt every tussock or bush in a small area but do not cover so much ground. I had one of each of these for several years and, between them, they didn't miss much.

It is important to have your dogs under control. I have already described how an untrustworthy dog can easily ruin future drives. There are other reasons. On one shoot where I pick-up there is hardly a drive where the picking-up does not involve handling dogs very close to a road. The A45, the A11 to Norwich and many others go through the shoot. I nearly always

end up hunting a dog along the hedges or verges of these roads. This must be done with extreme care and only with a dog that I am certain will stop as soon as I blow the stop whistle. I have only one dog which I can really trust. She will stop even when she is on a runner so I hunt her on her own when I am working along the side of these main roads. No running pheasant is worth the life of a dog and no reasonable host or gun would expect you to get a runner which could put a dog in danger.

My dogs must be enthusiastic hunters. They must persevere and try hard all day long. Some dogs will give up after a while and start looking at their handlers for instructions or cocking their legs on every bush. These dogs are exasperating and very exhausting to their handler who has constantly to encourage them. All dogs must learn to use their own initiative at times. There is a wide spectrum between initiative and control. We, as handlers, ask a lot of our dogs. One minute we want perfect control and handling, the next, when the dog is out of sight, we want him to use his own initiative and find runners without chasing unshot game. Dogs must be brave. They must face thick cover. Those which prink around the edge of brambles, nettles and all other forms of nasty cover are useless. Wounded birds will always try to tuck themselves into cover to hide and dogs must be prepared to go in after them.

Some dogs are naturally better game-finders than others and, obviously, you need dogs with 'good noses'. You can improve the way they use their noses in training by hiding dummies in thick cover and never making retrieves too easy for them. However, no training can alter the fact that some have a more acute sense of smell. These dogs are very useful but I often find that they are harder to train because their noses tell them everything and they think they need no further help from their handler.

The qualities, therefore, needed in a good picking-up dog are: an enthusiasm to hunt; a good nose; reasonable marking ability; initiative and a fair amount of control. Many excellent picking-up dogs would not make trial dogs because they might not be steady enough or sharp enough on the whistle, or perhaps they 'squeak' a bit or crush the odd strong cock runner. However, dogs with the qualities that I have listed can be useful to any shoot and give pleasure to their handlers. If anyone has a dog which is a steady 'peg' dog, good hunting dog, good trialling dog and good picking-up dog, it is probably a 'dog of a lifetime' and he wants to enjoy it while he has it. A dog's working life is, sadly, all too short.

Positioning

I have mentioned briefly where the picker-up ought to stand. This, of course, varies enormously according to the terrain, the weather and several other factors. He needs to see where wounded birds go. This is not always easy but, if he keeps going to the same shoot, he should learn the flight patterns of the birds and the places that they like to get to if they can. If I am picking-up in

Picker-up in an awkward situation with the sun

woodland I try to position myself in a clearing or where the trees are fairly thinly spread. The more open sky there is above, the easier it is to follow the direction of the birds and get some idea where they are going to land. If at all possible, I prefer to be on the outside of a wood, at least 30yd from it. From this vantage point I can get a good mark on any birds coming down inside. On a shoot on more open ground, the birds can fan out over a huge area, and go long distances, especially on windy days.

It is necessary to have several pickers-up to cover all the ground and, even then, they must be prepared to walk a long way for birds. It is never easy to tell whether birds have been hit or not unless you are close to the guns and can see them flinch in the air. They can fix their wings and glide on a long way and then suddenly fall dead. If they have a leg down or a wing knocked up it is obvious, but if there are no such signs, you just have to try and follow them and notice if they wobble in the air, slow down or go in an unexpected direction. You must not fall into the trap of thinking that they must be hurt if they trip up on landing. Tired birds will do this and every picker-up knows how easy it is to pick a tired bird. They do not want to get up and fly again if they have just been over the guns.

It can be very frustrating not to be able to communicate with the guns if you are a long way back. If you go off after a bird which is going to be a strong runner, you will almost certainly not notice others which probably land close by. The guns will think that you have spotted them but, if your eyes are fixed on a runner disappearing into the distance, you cannot observe anything else that is going on at the same time. You often find yourself in an awful dilemma as to whether to try and watch every bird down, or go for one which, from bitter experience, you know will be lost unless you go immediately. A walkie-talkie helps communication between pickers-up and the line of guns and often saves the former a great deal of effort. Nothing is more annoying than tiring yourself and your dogs after a drive searching for a bird that has already been picked.

It is often impossible to pick-up immediately after one drive because the birds have fallen into the next or an even later drive. This often causes runners to be lost. It also causes confusion when beaters' dogs go through picking birds. The poor pickers-up are left to try to work out what is left. This often means that your dogs are hunting for non-existent birds as beaters seem no better than guns at adding up.

I have seen enthusiastic pickers-up put themselves into situations where they cannot avoid pegging tired birds. This is a great pity and wasteful for the shoot. If you are on the edge of a covert where all the birds are going to land after a drive, it is extremely important that you are certain if there are seriously wounded birds in that covert. Nothing is easier than to put the dogs in and bring out bird after bird. If examined, very few of these will show any evidence of having been shot. In this situation, I try to mark the wounded birds as accurately as possible and then go into the covert quietly and only let one dog hunt close to me. The other occasion when I like to work with extreme care is after the last drive of the day if I am picking-up in a covert where the birds roost. If it is late in the afternoon the dogs can do more harm than good scaring birds that are thinking about going to bed.

Sometimes shoots end the day with a duck drive. This, necessarily, involves putting your dogs into cold water afterwards to retrieve the ducks. Sometimes they are wounded and keep diving whenever the dogs get near them. The dogs often have to swim around for ages to get these ducks and they get very cold. A picker-up should always take a towel and dry the dogs at the end of the day. He should never leave the poor animals shivering in the back of the car while he goes off to have a good meal. Dogs are expensive to buy, but your own good dogs are priceless. They will go on trying their hardest for you forever, so it is important to look after them well; they deserve it.

Young Dogs

In a young dog's first season it is important not to give him too much work. He has to start learning his 'trade' at this stage but, if he is overworked, he may become 'hot' and unsteady and, soon, out of control. Alternatively, if he is asked endlessly to hunt for non-existent or very doubtful pheasants he may lose his initial enthusiasm altogether. I try to drop a bird for a young dog occasionally so that he is successful. I prefer to take a young puppy to his first shoot where I am not officially picking-up. I can then concentrate on the puppy. He can sit in the line with a gun, and I can send him for a few selected retrieves that I know are not beyond his capabilities.

My final plea is that nobody starts picking-up without, first, learning how to dispatch game. My husband is a veterinary surgeon and feels strongly that breaking the birds' necks is very much more efficient than hitting them over the head with any form of priest. Anyone who feels that he cannot break necks of birds should buy a game dispatcher purpose-made.

Clothing

My advice on clothing is simply that it should be warm and waterproof and your boots should fit well. Your feet will suffer badly if you spend the whole day walking across sticky ploughed fields in boots that are either too big or too small. A previous writer on this subject stated that a picker-up should wear a hat and overtrousers. The photo on p000 illustrates the image that this conjured up in the mind of one of my more disreputable picking-up friends!

Picking-up, as a hobby, can be great fun. It is rarely dull. Even when you are standing, waiting for a drive, unexpected things can happen. I have watched all sorts of wildlife extremely close to me: weasels hunting; a kingfisher by a brook; a whole flock of long-tailed tits in a wood and many other things which I might not otherwise have seen. Life is normally too busy for there to be time to stand in a wood or by a hedge and just watch what is going on.

I have made countless mistakes when I have been picking-up. I have committed nearly all the sins that I have told others not to commit in this chapter. Keepers, hosts and guns are, however, very forgiving, and fear of not doing a good job should not prevent anyone from taking up the sport of picking-up. Anyone with good, well-trained, gundogs can be useful to a shoot and he will never regret the day that he goes to a keeper and asks if he can help with the picking-up.

Rough Shooting

VERONICA HEATH

Veronica Heath has been an enthusiastic amateur gundog handler on shoots in Northumberland since childhood. She beats and picks-up with a labrador and a spaniel and spends three weeks every August picking up grouse on Allenheads moor. She is a freelance journalist and author of several books, including A Dog at Heel *published in October, 1987 which dealt specifically with beating, picking-up and retrieving work. For eight years she has been a Country Diarist for the* Guardian. *She is also a keen foxhunter and deer stalker. She is married to a solicitor and has four children.*

Three inches of snow outside the drifts, drooping trees with skeletal branches and from a tangle of spent undergrowth in the hedgerow a liver-and-white back and a flashing tail burrows and is gone – and in that instant the magical clatter of our startled quarry. A golden cock pheasant with frantic beating wings is struggling to rise, catching the wind current he is airborne to his doom, a gun cracks and he topples earthwards. My eyes are trained on the plunging canine in the dyke bottom, will she stop or will she chase . . . a small, brown head thrusts through the brambles and waits, poised, ecstatic, watching. That little dog to me was poetry in motion. Shall I ever forget that heart-stopping moment, one of the outstanding incidents of early life, when the world and all it contained appeared larger than it does now and that solitary performance a miracle of training? I might go back to the same surroundings, to the same quarry and adopt the same methods, but it would be different. I can remember, but I cannot again experience, that glorious youthful feeling of enterprise, ambition and then, realisation.

Rough shooting with Papa on Fenrother moor was vintage stuff. Field craft and observation, silence and stealth was the name of the game. Irascible in old age, that little springer bitch was nevertheless brilliant in her prime and to me fell the task of handling her. As a small child I remember using a terrier, a useful canine on a rough shoot and I loved the rabbits which shot out of the whins on the fell and gave the guns a sporting chance. So I progressed to a proper gundog, without which no rough shoot is worthy of the name. A wonderful emancipation for me that spaniel, for there is a limit

Not all dogs care for the unusual flavour of a woodcock

to a teenager's enthusiasm for beating and carrying game. She opened the door to years of fun and good sport with a succession of gundogs, many of them, alas, lesser characters than she.

What is Rough Shooting?

The term rough shooting covers various forms of sport but it really implies those forms of shooting which do not entail the set party. It is now frequently referred to as 'walked-up' shooting. So you cannot say there are no beaters, implying driven game, because beaters can be very much part of the scene on a rough shoot. Not strictly necessary, but nonetheless useful, especially when the beater, like me, is also the dog-handler. The term also covers solitary hedgerow shooting, dog and man alone. We sit out for pigeons and stalk duck on an overgrown river which runs through our ground and all these activities are loosely embraced by the term, rough shooting. This form of shooting stirs the old primeval instincts of pot-hunting, of small but magnificent triumphs and, perhaps best of all, it commands a combination of loyalty, zeal and intelligence which is an efficient gundog. Grouse, pheasant, partridge, snipe, woodcock, duck, hare, pigeon and the rabbit are all legitimate quarry.

A Suitable Dog

In this form of shooting, as in no other, there is no ideal breed of gundog. Perhaps a spaniel, or an agile labrador or that incomparable all-rounder, one of the hunt, point, retrieve breeds, the German short or wirehaired pointer or the Brittany spaniel. The cocker spaniel is making a come-back and must certainly not be forgotten. Any one of these breeds will do the job provided that they are correctly educated and handled. A dog for a rough shoot is expected to work for what he gets, he will not stand about like a chorus in an opera waiting for birds to come over his head to drop where he can easily mark. He will need to use his legs as Nature intended and will not be carried about from drive to drive in a vehicle. The essential thing is that he should find the game for his master, this is his job and, unlike other forms of shooting, no one else will do this for him. Rough shooting without a dog is possible, but impractical. It becomes more a form of stalking game than walking it up; much less fun and not so lucrative. But in this form of shooting, more than in any other, the quality of the gundog is paramount; if he is undisciplined the game will flee before him, often so far in advance that the gun may not even be aware that it has been present. I would rather work the hedgerows and the root fields with our miniature dachshund than a wild gundog.

It is desirable for the rough-shooter's dog to retrieve the game as well as inducing it to become airborne within range of his master's gun. But it is not essential. For years I worked two dogs, a spaniel to flush and a labrador at heel to pick-up and it worked very well. Better to have two dogs which understand their basic work and execute it correctly than one which confuses the issue and starts to make a nonsense of it. It is exceedingly difficult to keep a spaniel steady to flush if he has been encouraged to retrieve cripples the moment they hit the ground. I find it difficult to keep my spaniel steady, so what of the man who carries the gun? Of course it can be done, much depends upon the character of the dog. However, a newcomer to rough shooting would be wise to train his first dog, initially, to hunt and to flush correctly and to ask a friend along whose canine companion would fill in with the retrieving work. Here and there you do find a dog which will hunt and yet be steady enough not to run in and chase when the guns are walking up in line but they are few and usually such treasures, especially if they are spaniels, will be well past middle age.

I am strongly of the opinion that too many modern gundogs suffer from lack of basic intelligence. Too many spaniels particularly are so highly bred with emphasis on speed and style and a pedigree ridden with field trial champions that their commonsense has suffered. The average amateur finds it almost impossible to control a hot-headed, long-legged springer which lacks brains. A dog with limited capabilities of understanding is prevented from realising that what is right now may be quite wrong ten minutes later under different circumstances. Taught to flush rabbits and running pheasants from thick cover which entails a short chase to put them out, he does not understand why he may not do the same in a field of roots. Rabbit scent inspires a spaniel to ignore all obstacles and discomfort. So intelligence is essential for the rough-shooter's dog. Most breeds can be trained to do one or two things passably well, constant repetition should ensure this. But the all-round dog must use his brain to understand his master's differing needs, for no day rough shooting is similar to another and unexpected situations constantly arise. An intelligent dog will learn more quickly by experience and will make fewer mistakes.

Labradors and Retrievers

Labradors and golden retrievers do seem to have the edge over the spaniel clan when it comes to brains. Hence the fact that these breeds are both very popular family dogs today. Labradors have also been bred smaller during the past twenty years and the old argument that the breed were too cumbersome and heavy to push game out of thickets is not so relevant today. The thick double coat is being bred out of the working strains too, the idea originally being that the dense otter jacket protected the labrador when he had to retrieve in icy water.

My present labrador is of the modern type, bought from a local keeper as a puppy. An active, fast dog she is tremendously agile and will go over or through a hedgerow or a taut wire fence with a retrieve in her mouth with absolutely no fuss. She will also go along a bank or a stone dyke like a stoat. Not quite as enthusiastic as the spaniel when it comes to brambles but if game is afoot she will persist in her work. I would rather use a biddable small labrador for flushing game than a headstrong spaniel. This particular labrador did not start any training until she was a year old and on one occasion during her first season picking-up she was sent out for an easy bird and started back with it when another, apparently dead bird got up and started legging it to the nearest ditch. She sized up the situation and went after the cripple without dropping the corpse she already had. Having stopped the wounded bird she spent a long time trying to work out how she was expected to get both back to me. Admittedly she was naughty to have been distracted by the second bird but I thought she displayed intelligence in her work. Most young dogs would have dropped the first pheasant and abandoned it for the runner.

The most widely accepted theory is that the original labradors were brought over about 1800 in the boats which carried salted cod from Newfoundland to Poole harbour. They were strong swimmers and probably carried the fishermen's ropes ashore onto the shelving beaches. The golden retrievers' ancestors were sheep-dogs of the Caucasus and were reputed to be so faithful to their charges that in winter they were left with their own cache of food to guard the flocks until the shepherds returned to them in spring. Can you imagine any modern dog doing that today? I doubt if we could find an individual with the intelligence or the tenacity of character. Golden retrievers are essentially slower dogs at work than labradors and spaniels and not so well suited to rough shooting, although I am sure there are exceptions. I do think that the character of the countryside today is not conducive to a large dog for rough shooting. We are constantly beset by tight-stranded fences frequently topped with barbed wire, cattle grids, stone walls, highways, heavy ploughed fields, pig netting and even electric fencing.

HPRs

The hunt, point, retrieve breeds are ideal rough-shooting dogs. The little Brittany spaniel seems to me the epitome of the 'one man, one dog' combination, a spaniel, pointer and retriever all in one attractive package. On the Continent and in America the breed is popular as a family pet as well as a working dog and those I have seen in the field display considerable intelligence. It is widely believed that the Brittany originated from a small, short-tailed, liver-and-white spaniel indigenous to the Brittany region of France. During the second half of the nineteenth century this spaniel became interbred with English, Irish and Gordon setters and pointers which were brought to France by English landowners and gamekeepers and subsequently left with local farmers until the next shooting season.

This theory would account for the size, scenting and pointing ability found in the breed today. German shorthaired and wirehaired pointers must be a joy for the one-man hunter, but demand careful, experienced handling. The wildest dogs I have ever seen were GSPs and they were tall, rangy canines which hunted over the horizon like lunatics when not on a rope. When well handled they are definitely the tops for rough shooting and for walked-up partridge and grouse. The dog's every stride is made in readiness to halt, to turn, to swing the questing nose towards any change in the flavour of the air, to unravel the eddies in the wind currents. To achieve all this at an unslackened pace is an achievement of precision and beauty conveyed by the economical rhythmical, rippling gallop which all these dogs possess.

Pointers work well on partridges and with changing agricultural practices the stubbles left by the combine harvesters have led to a return to traditional shooting over dogs. The dogs must quarter intelligently and systematically, always working upwind lest they overrun birds and put them up too soon. On scenting game they halt far enough away to avoid disturbance, yet close enough to be sure that game is actually there. This process which sounds simple demands a keen nose, stamina, concentration and instant reflex action. The breed originated in Germany, probably from a cross of the bloodhound on the old Spanish pointer. Once a devotee of the HPR breeds, individuals tend to stick to them. On the Continent, pointers are used to retrieve, to hunt thickets for woodcock and pheasants and to act as general-purpose dogs with the result that they often have more intelligence than their English cousins.

Spaniels

Springer spaniels are admirably suited to rough shooting because their size enables them to get through and under thick cover more easily than a bigger dog and they have such a fervid enthusiasm for hunting that they face any obstacle. But I do not believe that their intelligence compares with that of some other breeds. Most of the ratings and beatings that spaniels get from irate owners are useless for the simple reason that many of them have not sufficient intelligence to know why they are being chastised. I would venture to suggest that not ten spaniels in a hundred which are used for hunting hedgerows and thick cover are steady enough for any other kind of shooting. Where are the reliable, plodding Clumbers which we used to see on our rough shoots? The only ones I have seen this last ten years were on the show bench. A team of Clumber spaniels was introduced to Sandringham by King Edward VII who used them to flush pheasants from the rhododendrons. In the years before gunpowder, long-tailed springer spaniels were employed to spring or flush game into nets and springing game to the gun was not very different.

Changes have been man-made and man-felt and springers today have

The English springer spaniel shelters under a beech: many rough shooters' first choice of dog

progressed from stolid, common stock to sensitive thoroughbred dogs. The breed is really an offshoot of the field spaniel, a breed of old standing which, after a period of decline, is now coming into its own again. The man, or woman, who wants a springer as a rough-shooting companion must take extra care to check his puppy's credentials. Some of the keepers on our northern grouse moors breed a good strain, small and sturdy. Check parents carefully, see both at work if possible. The cocker spaniel is the comedian of the gundog world and some good workers are now being bred for shooting. The long ears seem rather an encumbrance but their diminutive size is no deterrent to good work. The ones I know personally have also managed to retain the courage and the sense of humour for which the breed has been immortalised. But a cocker needs a firm trainer's hand if he is to become a companion worthy of the gun. Again, check credentials carefully before buying a puppy.

Training

The secret of a useful working dog for a rough shoot is discipline. This is based on a number of words of command which convey instant meaning. No dog, of any breed, should be introduced to battle conditions until he has become absolutely reliable to voice or whistle, free from chase, dropping, or at best halting, to shot, and walking to heel without any attempt to leave until told to do so. A tall order? Yes, maybe, but it really is the only way to achieve a first-class rough-shooting gundog.

Amateur handlers will need to work out a sensible code of behaviour for

Steadiness training in the rabbit pen will pay dividends later

the young dog in the home environment. A few simple rules should be made and adhered to for the whole of the dog's working life. It is not the slightest use spending half an hour a day training for steadiness and then allowing the children to take the dog for an unsupervised walk amongst game. Even in the country there are places to exercise where there is no game and those of our comrades who live in towns need not feel that their gundog training facilities are inadequate. The park or the beach are excellent places where a gundog can run free without risk of detriment to his training. Wild walks are ruination to a keen dog. Once a spaniel has got his head right down to ground game and has tasted the illicit joys of chasing for himself no chastisement will break him of the habit. Every puppy must be given the opportunity to run around, to use his nose and investigate every scent but he should be aware that master is at hand and he is under supervision. However delicious the scent may be, he may sniff to his heart's content, but never touch. *Never* let the dog chase birds or run fur by sight. He must learn that scent of game is the gun's concern as well as his own and it is his job to pass on the exciting information that birds are at hand. Yours is a partnership and he is merely the junior partner – never let him forget it.

The check cord is no substitute for slack supervision and it is only effective as a preliminary measure and should not be necessary at all. A spaniel which quarters naturally is valuable, they do not all have this aptitude although it is not difficult to teach it. A natural beating dog will work out to right and then to left of his handler, turning naturally and crossing in front. Set a limit for the distance the dog is free to go out from you. His place is anywhere and everywhere within a 30yd semicircle ahead. That is his territory. The ideal is to have the dog constantly active, vitally interested but fixed by an invisible cord to his master's belt. I am not only referring to spaniels working on a rough shoot, this applies to labradors and golden retrievers too.

Gundogs are naturally servile creatures, they like to be dominated by a human and the happiest gundogs are those which are under control and serving master correctly. This characteristic allows you to fix the invisible cord. It is companionship to some degree but it is less and more. Mutual respect perhaps, so that each respects the other's expertise and builds on it to make a team. During every walk and training foray never let the dog go beyond 30yd without a whistle or a call. Gradually he will come to expect it and it will become second nature to pause, to turn and to check where master is. Never relax vigil and I promise you that it will be worthwhile. It is the purest joy to take a dog out onto stubble, hedgerow and into thick cover and to work him in the growing confidence that the penny has dropped at last and he will always turn and respond just as a good beating dog should. Even after this satisfactory state of affairs has been reached, whistle him across from time to time to let him know that you are vigilant. If the dog misses a gorse bush or a clump of rushes and you want it investigated, then see that he does it for you. Insist that he comes across and hunts it out. Remind him that his job is to find the game, yours is merely to shoot it.

Work on open pasture and stubble fields which host coveys of partridges and squatting hares must follow hedgerow work. Postpone running him under these testing conditions until the dog has acquired a confirmed range and is steady to ground game. Roots and game crops should not pose a problem but insist that the dog works every inch thoroughly. A small spaniel can be difficult to see in a tall crop, so do not let him take advantage.

A gundog will soon learn to differentiate between wildfowling and other forms of shooting, where he must remain seated until the drive is over. I use my spaniels picking-up on grouse moors here in Northumberland and they sit for half an hour behind the butts without any trouble. It is all a build-up of experience. A good dog, especially a labrador, quickly learns that incoming duck come into the wind. Rarely will a dog give trouble about retrieving from water but a cripple in an overgrown reed bed or marsh can be very difficult to find. Moreover, winged duck are capable of running great distances in a short space of time. So the dog will often need to be sent quickly to the fall – a short step to running-in. Never let him go unbidden, make him look to you for the order. A rough-shooting dog must retrieve willingly from water and the best way to teach a youngster is to encourage him to follow an older dog into shallow water.

Working two dogs on a rough shoot is much more demanding than a one-dog, one-man relationship. I have noticed how much better some dogs work when there are no others to distract or to interfere with the work. Dogs can be jealous of rival workers. So it is unwise to rush into the two-dog situation and I never understand the man with a good gundog bitch which is coming along nicely who decides to breed from her before she has had time to get her act together. Within eighteen months he has two novice dogs on his hands. A rough-shooting dog can reach three or four years old before he comes to his best work, sometimes longer if he does not get a lot of work.

With an abundance of obstacles now on every rough shoot ranging from hairy hedges to tight-stranded wire, the gun must teach his young dog to cope with these hazards himself. It is ridiculous to lift a young dog over a wall or to coax him between wires. You may be sure that he will be agile enough in getting over or through any obstacle on the hot scent of a runner. Teach the dog to jump, introduce him to small obstacles at a comparatively young age and use the command 'over'. A puppy can be taken on interesting walks where he will meet natural hazards and he will soon learn to use his initiative by working out a route for himself. Cattle grids can be nasty; I always take trouble to show the dogs how treacherous they can be and get an experienced dog to show a pup the way round. A dog which has learnt to jump freely with maximum propulsion will soon learn to clear a wire fence without damage to the undercarriage. Gundogs vary in their development and some learn quicker than others to cope with natural rough-shooting hazards. This applies to all stages of the training experience programme and must be accepted.

Before deciding upon the breed of dog you are going to buy for rough shooting it is a wise plan to join the line of beaters on a local shoot. Watch the dogs carefully and ask yourself which is the type you have in mind for yourself? Go for the dog which works thoroughly without pottering or rushing about with his head in the air, looks to his master for orders and finds and flushes game without chasing. Ask where the dog came from, who bred him and who trained him. Get a picture in your mind of what you want and take time to find it. There are plenty of good dogs about and they do not necessarily have to have field trial credentials in their pedigrees. To most amateurs a pedigree form is so much paperwork. There will likely be no need to travel half across the British Isles to find a puppy. Look in your own parish on the local shoots and see which of your shooting friends has a useful bitch. Or if you know a good gundog trainer, ask him to find you a suitable dog, I know several people who have done this with success. A local man will not risk his reputation by selling an unsuitable dog to a client in the neighbourhood. If you decide to buy a trained dog, and there is no disgrace at all attached to doing so, then fix up several lessons with the trainer and learn how to handle him. For a novice who plans to carry a gun rough shooting this is a sensible plan for a first dog. Time enough later to train on the next one yourself.

Brent

JOHN HUMPHREYS

I was determined to pass on the memory of my famous Drake in a more tangible way than by just thinking of him each time I saw the lonely willow tree by the river which would mark his grave when his time came. I had bred from him with a lovely little bitch, Sally, which belonged to a keeper friend Les King of Roxton in Bedfordshire. My end of the bargain was pick of the litter in the hope of carrying on where Drake had left off, for with another dog even approaching his all-round ability, my shooting would be on a safe footing for at least another decade.

The deed was done and again I set off to view the litter, another journey full of hope but tinged with anxiety in case I got it wrong. Had I not had the pick of the litter with the formidable Cassius, and look how he had turned out? Again the black tide of rotund little puppies flowed round my ankles as the barn door was opened and again I picked a chubby little dog which seemed to be of a no-nonsense and fairly robust disposition. Again we embarked on the sea of dog ownership. All those mistakes made in the past were behind us, it was the chance for a fresh start and in how many human affairs can that be said, I wonder?

Both parents were of impeccable stock and there was little this time surely that could go wrong. The new boy was from the start a promising prospect, being of a friendly disposition, willing and eager to please. His boisterousness reminded us of some things about puppy ownership which we had forgotten. Choice plants were bitten off, quite stout shrubs pruned down to ground level and any object from a plastic bucket to a broom left lying around was either dragged into a quiet corner and systematically demolished, or embossed with tiny toothmarks and embellished with a daintily scolloped edge. The pond was daily emptied of its plants as Brent took a running jump and leapt into the water in an entirely satisfying but completely destructive manner.

Drake, being tolerant, did not mind being ambushed from the cover of the herbaceous border or having needle teeth clamped onto his ear as he made a lordly progress up the path. He was less certain about being pounced on when he lay snoozing in the sun and was even obliged to administer a sharp lesson about the inviolability of one's feeding bowl and the respect that is due to elders and betters, but by and large the relationship was as good as you might expect between father and son. They lay together on the grass like two ill-matched, anthracite bookends in a sunny spot by the willow tree.

Early training we took at a leisurely pace with none of that sense of urgency felt by a one-dog man. Drake had a season left in him so we could afford to take our time. Two or three minutes a day were enough to move him gently along the paths he was eventually to follow, but soon I came to realise that all was far from well. After a few weeks Brent seemed unwilling, or unable, to jump the most modest obstacle. There was a noted stiffness in his hindquarters after a spell of lying down, even on warm days, for all the world like a dog of nine years instead of nine months. I guessed at a muscle strained in the rough and tumble of kennel play, but time passed and the condition did not ease and, still unwilling to face the possibility of anything sinister, I took him to the vet for a routine X-ray on his hips.

I returned on Friday evening to collect him and it was to prove a harrowing experience. Our vet is a good dog man but he needed to tell me nothing after he had shown me the plates. The dog had virtually no hip joints at all. Where the deep sockets housing the heads of the femurs should have been there was flat bone: it was one of the worst cases of hip dysplasia you could imagine. Both parents had been believed clear of the scourge, but it has been known to skip generations. His prospects as a gundog living the sort of life I had in mind for him were as good as nil. Even as a household pet they were little better as he might have lasted for three years or so before acute rheumatoid arthritis would have been the end of him.

There was no choice, in spite of the complex but uncertain operations which the vet offered me, the decision was as obvious as it was painful. I emerged from the surgery holding a collar and lead, a tear in the eye and no dog. My children waiting in the car could not be swayed by cold logic and it was some weeks before the family became reconciled to the loss. Already we had come to love him and regard him as a member of the family and all the good sense in the world does not reconcile you to such a loss. 'Brothers and sisters I bid you beware, of giving your heart to a dog to tear.'

The dreadful disease was then at its peak and few gundogs were entirely free of it, the result of selective breeding for too long and the totally unrealistic breed standards for show. Today things are easier and commonsense has taken a hand. HD-free has become an expectation and there are some vets who will issue a certificate to that effect. Such thoughts were cold enough comfort to me at the time, still nursing my loss.

Such was the tale and a brief one it is, of the shortest-lived of the many dogs I have owned. I include it as a lesson to those who rush too eagerly into buying without obtaining a proper assurance that the HD genes and, come to that, those of PRA are not present in breeding stock. Oddly enough the litter brothers and sisters of Brent all lived long and happy lives without a hint of disability.

The Field Trial

JOHN HALSTEAD

John Halstead is a top, professional gundog trainer who, together with his wife Sandra, owns the famous Drakeshead gundog kennels. He has been competing in field trials for over twenty years. During the last thirteen years, the Drakeshead kennel has 'made up' fourteen field trial champions – all labradors – six of which are still living with the Halsteads. Two of them have won the IGL Retriever Championship, Shot winning it with Sandra and John making history with Breeze by winning the championship three years in succession, 1985, 1986 and 1987.

John came close to winning the coveted double when, after winning the 1987 Retriever Championship, he won third place with his English springer spaniel Dash at the 1987 Spaniel Championship.

John and Sandra spend the summer months at their trout fishery and training young dogs. John enjoys shooting over his dogs and picking-up with a team of retrievers and the occasional spaniel. He is a firm believer that there is no better finishing school for the retrieving breeds than a season picking-up.

What is a field trial? And what is it that makes competitors travel great distances, stretch their purse strings to extremes, push their nerves to near breaking point repeatedly returning home disappointed in their dog's performance or cursing themselves for their own failings?

On the face of things you would be right in assuming that they were completely mad and quite honestly at times the handlers themselves would agree with your verdict for to take part in a field trial, you must have what I call the 'rubber ball temperament', you must keep bouncing back. You must

137

be your own critic and never be totally satisfied with your dogs or your own performance. For I can honestly say that I have never competed in a field trial, even when I was the winner, and not found, after analysing the event, quite a few things I should or could have done better.

All field trials are run under Kennel Club Field Trial Rules and Regulations. The Kennel Club says in its introduction:

(a) A field trial is a meeting for the purpose of holding competitions to assess the work of gundogs in the field, with dogs working on live, unhandled game where game may be shot.

(b) Game that has been handled in any way either dead or alive may not be used for testing dogs in any part of a field trial except that it may be used in conduct of a water test or a test to the award of a Show Gundog Working Certificate.

(c) Societies which are registered with the Kennel Club and which have been so authorised may organise field trials. A licence must be obtained from the Kennel Club for every trial in accordance with the procedure set out in these regulations.

(d) Any field trial not licensed by the Kennel Club is liable to be deemed an unrecognised canine event.

(e) Field trials shall be conducted in accordance with the field trial regulations.

The regulations then go on to describe the 'stakes' in each field trial in more detail:

(a) A field trial may consist of one or more stakes which are separate competitions at that trial.

(b) Stakes may be run for any of the four sub-groups of gundogs recognised by the Kennel Club under the appropriate regulations and in accordance with the appropriate guide to their conduct.

(c) The four sub-groups are as follows:
    (i) Retrievers and Irish water spaniels.
    (ii) Sporting spaniels other than Irish water spaniels.
    (iii) Pointers and setters.
    (iv) Breeds which hunt, point and retrieve.

(d) The following are definitions of certain stakes:
    (i) *Open* A stake in which dogs have the opportunity of gaining a qualification (whole or part) for the title of field trial champion or for entering the championship or champion stake for its breed and in which

English springer 'springing' pheasants

'The spaniel can take on anything required, hunting, retrieving, working in water and as a family pet'

The whistle is the trainer's friend

John Halstead taking a retrieve from Drummer at the CLA Game Fair at Tatton Park

entry is open to all dogs of a specified breed or breeds. It may be limited to a prescribed number of runners in which case these shall be decided by a draw where preference must be given to previous performance.

(ii) *All Age*   A stake which is open to all dogs of a specified breed or breeds without restriction as to their age but which may be restricted by any other conditions which may be determined by the Society.

(iii) *Novice*   A stake which is confined to dogs which have not gained the following awards. First or second or third in open stakes or first or two seconds in other stakes.

(iv) *Puppy*   A stake which is confined to dogs whelped not earlier than 1st January in the year preceding the date of the field trials. For such stakes run in January a dog which was a puppy in the previous year shall be deemed to be still a puppy.

(e) Other stakes may, with Kennel Club approval, be promoted by the Society but all stakes must be clearly defined in the schedule.

The regulations carry on with application and documentation, then go into great detail about appointment of judges, entries and so on. But a very important point is the guide to the conduct of field trials.

The Competition

'These notes are designed as a guide to the organisers of field trials and competitors to assist judges in selecting their best shooting dogs. No judge should accept an invitation to judge trials and no competitor should enter trials unless he is fully conversant with the field trial regulations and has studied this guide. The secretary of a field trial should ensure that each of the judges at a field trial has a copy of the guide available.

A field trial should be run as nearly as possible to an ordinary day's shooting where the judges could select the best shooting dogs.' The last sentence of some twenty-odd words could be quickly read and hardly noticed but in my opinion they should be printed in bold capitals in the regulations and engraved into the memories of judges and handlers alike. In those few words everything that matters has been condensed for the end-product of a field trial must be a top-class shooting dog, the breed relative to its function in the shooting field. The task of the judges is to find a dog which on the day pleases them most by the quality of his work from the shooting point of view. They should take natural game finding to be of the first importance in field trials. In fact if we look at the credit points of all the gundog breeds they are very, very similar. For instance natural game-finding ability; nose; marking; drive; style; quickness in gathering game; control; quietness in the handling, retrieving and delivery. There are slight variations for spaniels, bird dogs and the HPRs. They incorporate ground treatment, which is termed as quartering or pattern and they are judged on their actual ground treatment which plays the major part of a questing dog's duties.

We vary a little bit on the pointers and setters for they have a different carriage and only quest for gamebirds. In fact when you look at all the breeds their shoulders or their structure over the generations of breeding have been developed for their task in the field. For instance, a retriever's shoulders are so placed that he carries his head almost horizontal with his body because most of his work is actually retrieving so he needs powerful shoulders and also he must have a carriage where he can put his head down to hunt. Now with the English springer spaniel, 90 per cent of his work is done with his head almost totally on the ground hunting, so his shoulders have to be placed in such a way as to allow his head to be carried comfortably when near the ground.

The bird dogs are again different for they must have a very high head carriage to allow them to hunt their ground at great speed taking in air scent. The pointers and setters also have another requirement. The second dog must back the first dog when he is on point. That means that when the first dog finds birds and goes onto point the second dog must point the dog that is already on point. If the second dog is close by when birds are found and he creeps forward this is what we call 'trying to steal the point' and he would be severely penalised.

In the *Kennel Club Field Trial Rules and Regulations and Guide to Judges* the order of sending etc has been standardised so that at least all the judges follow the same procedure. In retriever trials, I should say more than any other trials, the actual judging is the making or breaking of the trial and at the end of the day you will hear competitors say, 'Why that was a marvellous trial, it did not need any judging for everything just fell into place'. Now that is a sure sign that those judges have managed the trial to perfection for it hinges on how the game is used and how the judges get together to say which dogs are to be sent.

If you were to ask me what should be the qualities of field-trial judges I would have to say that first and foremost they must be directly involved in the actual shooting field. Also they must have been involved in training and running dogs in competitions, for only then would they know how the competitors are feeling and how to judge them, if to make allowances or otherwise. Another main factor is that they must be decisive. For instance in a retriever

An attacking start while the judge makes notes

trial if you have three judges judging and they can't decide on which dog to send when there is a runner shot, then that indecision can mean failure or otherwise and at the end of the day it is the competitor who suffers.

When a dog is out hunting for a retrieve the judge has to decide on the amount of time to allow the dog to complete his task. If a dog is hunting with enthusiasm and looks as though he will be successful then I would allow him more time than a dog who was performing indifferently. In fact, a good yardstick is if a point has been reached and a dog could not be given any credit if he now found the retrieve, he should be called up. There are occasions when a handler has been told to call his dog up and at that moment the dog finds, in this case I would still have the dog marked as having failed, for once I have asked the handler to call up his dog I have ceased to judge that dog. The time factor is even more critical when a dog is being tried on a runner for if a dog is performing indifferently on a runner he should be called up promptly in order to give the second dog a chance.

By far the most distasteful task a judge has to perform is when he has to eliminate dogs. In the Kennel Club regulations there is a list of eliminating and major faults for each gundog group. Most of the eliminating faults apply to all the groups for example, hard mouth; whining or barking; running-in and chasing; out of control; failing to enter water; chasing game whilst retrieving. The spaniels and HPRs have two additional categories: missing game on the beat and not stopping to shot. The pointers and setters are not required to retrieve, therefore hard mouth, swimming and changing game whilst retrieving are not required but flushing upwind and blinking a point are eliminating faults for bird dogs. These set rules of eliminating and major faults are there to guide the judges and maintain a high standard of dog work.

They serve a second purpose in attempting to prevent hereditary faults getting into the breed such as hard mouth and whining which, once established, can take years of selective breeding to eradicate. Let us look at a few of the eliminating and major faults and see how the judges would assess them.

Hard Mouth

All game should be examined for signs of damage. Hard-mouthed dogs seldom give visible evidence of hardness. They will simply crush in one or both sides of the ribs, blowing up the feathers of the bird will not disclose the damage. Place the game on the palm of your hand, breast upwards, head forwards and feel the ribs with finger and thumb. They should be round and firm. If they are caved-in or flat, this is evidence of hard mouth. Be sure that the game reaches the other judges for examination. There should be no hesitation or sentiment with hard mouth, the dog should be discarded. Judges should always satisfy themselves that the damage done has been caused by the dog not by the shot or fall and in cases of doubt the benefit should be given to the dog. Handlers should be given the opportunity of inspecting the bird in the presence of the judges but the decision of the judges is final. At times the rump of a strong runner may be gashed and look ugly and care should be taken here as it may be the result of a difficult capture or lack of experience in mastering a strong runner by a young dog.

Whining

Whining is one of the most annoying habits that gundogs can develop and can be contagious to dogs in adjoining kennels. In the majority of cases it can be checked in early training, but with the remainder their excitable temperament is such that they begin to whine especially sitting at a peg while being shot over. Judges should discard dogs immediately for whining or barking. This should not be confused with the sighing or whistling noise that some dogs make when retrieving from water.

Changing Game

Retriever breeds are trained to assist the gun or shooting party to collect dead or wounded game. The guns and people picking-up have a rough idea of where the game is to be found but after an ill-trained dog has picked several retrieves and run off with them to change to another, then no one is sure where the game is to be found and inevitably game is lost.

Some people say that it shows intelligence if a dog is returning with a dead bird and he changes it for a bird that falls and runs. My reply to this type of logic is 'What happens when your dog is returning with a runner and another runner is shot, or a dog is swimming back with a live duck and another wounded duck falls close by?' In both cases the dog which leaves one for the other could end up with none.

Out of Control

A dog is out of control when the judges, through their experience, can be sure that the handler has completely lost contact with his dog and in most cases the dog will be disturbing ground and game.

Pegging

Pegging, ie deliberately catching unshot game, is a major fault and there is quite a bit of controversy around this fault, hence the word 'deliberately'. Again it is the experience of the judges which will enable them to assess if a dog is deliberately going in to catch live game or if a bird or rabbit is trapped in cover and the dog simply lifts it. Another point is that on some larger commercial shoots where they shoot several days per week then it is logical to assume that there must be quite a number of wounded birds on the ground. In fact a good maxim is, always judge people and their dogs as you would like to be treated yourself.

When we come to the actual running of the field trial, a friendly atmosphere and the smooth running of the event can be helped considerably or hindered by the attitude of the judges. In fact the trial should have the same atmosphere as a shooting day. So what can the judges do? First and foremost, introduce themselves to each other and their stewards. Then they should introduce themselves to the keeper and ask him about the game situation and decide amongst themselves how many retrieves to have in the first round. They must ask the keeper how many guns there are, and if the keeper has never organised a trial before, explain to him what is required from the trial point of view but stress that they will fit in with all his requirements as to the management of the day ahead. He is the steward of the beat, he will dictate the pace of his line of guns in a retriever trial and will decide on the ground to be used by spaniels, pointers and setters etc. If you can make a friend of the keeper then the day will run smoothly and you will have a marvellous sporting atmosphere. You should suggest to the keeper that the most experienced judge could have a word with the guns to explain what is required from the dogs' point of view. For instance, not to shoot game directly over a dog which is out working for a retrieve.

Pointer and Setter Trials

I have some very happy memories of training pointers up on the grouse moors where I used to live. The area I used was owned by the water authority and was neither shot nor keepered, therefore it could only support a very small

FTCH Drakeshead Luke negotiating a fence at the England v Wales working test

number of birds, in fact it was ideal for training bird dogs. After I had completed the early obedience lessons, had taught the dog to point caged pigeons and to be steady to a sprung pigeon, it was time to introduce him to the real thing to enable him to differentiate between quarry (in this case grouse) and a variety of other interesting smells such as hares, rabbits, larks etc. Up to now the pigeons that he had been taught to point also had my hand scent.

My wife, Sandra, would drive me over the moor and deposit me several miles away from home to enable me to work back with a pointer, with perhaps a couple of labradors at heel. I often gave the labradors the odd retrieve of a tennis ball in the heather while resting the pointer after a hard run. I cannot think of anything more exciting than when a dog finds birds, freezes instantly and awaits his boss coming onto the scene before being instructed to go forward from a pointing position towards the game.

Pointers and setters must have an incredible amount of stamina for when cast off, the dog's beat can be quite extensive depending on the terrain but he must always be able to be in contact with his handler. The dogs appear to flow like liquid over the ground using the wind to full advantage, then they find and freeze on point with the second dog backing the dog who has found his birds.

The pointer and setter field-trial season starts with the spring trials when dogs would be hunting mainly for partridge, then grouse trials in summer usually prior to 12 August followed in late September by pheasant hunting. The major events would be held in the few weeks prior to 12 August and on rare occasions, if game was to be shot, then the event would be held after 12 August.

There are two judges officiating at pointer and setter trials; in the champion stake they must both be on the A Panel. In open stakes they must both be panel judges, one of whom must be on the A Panel and in other stakes one at least must be on the A Panel.

Prior to the trial dogs are assigned numbers which are drawn randomly to determine which dogs shall hunt as a brace and the order of their running. The competition is not of the knock-out type and it is important for newcomers to appreciate that the competitors run with and not against one another. The judges will judge each brace together and after the first round the remaining dogs will be drawn again to run in pairs in the second round. During the stake the judges will be looking at the total quality of the dog's work and the way he quarters his ground; his ability to find birds; pace; style and steadiness. Natural backing and style on point would also be taken into consideration.

The dog should quarter with pace and style making good all his ground, working correctly to the wind, particularly if down wind or a cheek wind, showing gamebird finding ability, working naturally with the minimum of handling and working his point out freely. Dogs should be steady to fur and feather and should drop to shot and if a dog flushes gamebirds upwind he should be discarded, but if he is working downwind and flushes or on the first cast runs sideways into gamebirds and drops immediately and may have no chance to wind them these do not constitute an eliminating flush. When a dog has worked ground and gamebirds are proved to be left on the beat, that dog has missed gamebirds and should be eliminated. If gamebirds are found on ground which the dog should have worked but did not cover the judge should consider the circumstances before penalising the dog for faulty ground treatment (but not for missing gamebirds). A dog should also be discarded if after pointing gamebirds he leaves (blinks) the point and continues hunting.

Anyone who has had the opportunity of shooting over bird dogs would have to agree with me that it is a sport second to none especially on grouse where dogs are using their natural ability. The handler is applying his field craft and using his experience to work his dogs where they are likely to find birds or a quarry that is totally wild and living in its natural environment. Unfortunately these are also some of the reasons that restrict pointers and setters to the open spaces of vast acres of rolling downland or the grouse moors of the North of England and Scotland. They are certainly not the dogs for the rough shooter or the formal shoot. The HPR can partly fill this gap for a person who likes to shoot over a bird dog but has only rough shooting available to him. Like their title their duties are to quarter the ground, find, point and flush on command both gamebirds and ground game and after a successful shot to retrieve on command.

Retriever Trials

In retriever trials there is what is termed the three-judge system and the four-judge system. In the four-judge system the judges will judge in pairs so there is a right and left side of the line and two dogs under each couple of judges. For example, dogs 1 and 2 would be under the judges on the right and dogs 3 and 4 under the judges on the left-hand side, for in the body of the stake we always number from the right.

In the three-judge system the judges will be positioned left, centre and right. Each judge will usually have two guns shooting for him and he will normally place himself and his dogs between his guns. If there are extra guns then it should be decided which judge they are to shoot for. This will go a long way to avoiding two dogs being sent for the same game. The steward of the beat will be in charge of the line and dictate the pace of the line. Dogs will be asked to walk steadily at heel and sit quietly at drives. If the game situation permits, two retrieves will be requested under the first judge or pair of judges followed by one retrieve in the second round. The judges may then confer and discard any dogs they no longer require. The dog steward should be informed of any dogs eliminated or discarded for any reason and this will allow him to have the right dogs in line. The dog steward should be instructed to send in the second-round dogs when there is a vacancy in the line. Second-round dogs should have their opportunity to be tried against first-round dogs when the situation arises.

By far the best retriever trials, both from the competing and judging point of view, are what we term 'walking-up trials' where guns, judges, handlers

Flatcoat in action

and officials walk the ground in a long straight line and game is shot both in front of and behind the line. Both the dogs and handlers have to be capable of marking shot birds both in front and behind them, also from one end of the line to the other which can, in some cases, be a considerable distance. Two to three hundred yards is not uncommon particularly on the grouse moors in the North of England and Scotland where game is not so concentrated.

In the eastern counties, in Lincolnshire for example, where most of the trials are in sugar-beet, the line is generally shorter and more densely populated for there can be a great deal of game in a small acreage. Imagine the morning of the trial: the handlers' nerves are already starting to get the adrenalin moving for there are always quite a few unknown factors at every field trial. What will the scent be like? You may see one or two handlers throwing the odd tennis ball before the trial starts to confirm their thoughts on the matter. Some will be trying to acquire knowledge from the locals about the type of ground to be used. Are there a lot of hares? Will there be drives or walking-up etc? The more experienced handlers will also be getting a touch of nerves, but have long since decided that it is much easier to take things as they come and that if you have done your homework thoroughly then you and your dog will be able to cope with whatever situation arises during the trial.

During the trial successful dogs will have had the opportunity of three retrieves. It is during this period that the judges can assess the dogs. They can assess steadiness, their marking and natural game-finding ability, and gun sense, which is going straight to the area of the shot when ground game is shot. It is at this stage that the judges can probably eliminate quite a few dogs and decide which dogs they want to carry forward to the final placings which we call a 'run-off'. In the run-off each dog may be asked to pick four or five more retrieves. At this stage a dog may be stretched to such a degree that he may fail and be 'eye-wiped'. In this situation the dog would be penalised but could still feature in the final awards.

The dog steward will have been instructed by the judges to call out the numbers still required. This is when the trial really becomes a competition for during the preliminary rounds the judges will have assessed the general standards of the dogs and, depending on the quality of the scent or lack of it, they will know to what degree they can stretch their finalists.

I prefer to send all the dogs in the run-off in numerical order. This is by far the fairest way and handlers and spectators alike can see fair play. The only time I would deviate from this policy is when all the judges have agreed that they may want to see a particular dog handled or they may want to see a dog pick feather who has come through to the run-off on ground game. But I do not agree with favouring or shielding a dog that has done some very good work earlier in the stake.

The final placings of the trial require the judges to go through their books for the whole trial and what I would look for is the consistent 'A' dog. In my opinion the dog which has been consistent throughout the trial acquiring, say, eight As is better than a dog who has five As, two A+s and a B. In my book two excellent retrieves cannot cancel out a bad retrieve. The spectators quite often think that all the dogs in the run-off are starting on equal merit and when the final awards are read out they think perhaps that the first-placed dog should have been second but they have not had the judges' books to examine concerning the earlier retrieves and quite often the best dogs make everything look so easy.

I remember, on more than one occasion, when I was running FTCh Drakeshead Tinker who was a brilliant marker, being sent for an obvious runner. He would be out like lightning and pin-point the fall. On the way back with the bird I would quite often hear the judges say, 'The bird had not gone anywhere', and I would be thinking, 'No, but it would have done if the dog had not been such a good marker'. On the other hand, you may see a dog that was a bad marker take so much time in getting to the fall that by the time he got there the bird had gone to the end of the field. The dog would then put his nose down and make a really workmanlike job of it, and come up with the final result, getting the bird. Some judges would then credit this dog with a fantastic retrieve and give it an A+, whereas if that dog had got to the fall immediately the bird might not have had time to run. So the judges should see the whole picture and if the dog does not mark and makes a retrieve into a more difficult retrieve by not marking, he should be penalised rather than gain extra credit.

Thinking back over Breeze's field-trial career, and his incredible game-finding ability, he was at his best when conditions were at their worst and some of the top dogs in the country were finding scent so poor that runners did not seem to be pickable. That is what all judges should be looking for. A dog which performs his duties with the least assistance from his handler, possesses a natural game-finding ability, is a good marker and a persistent hunter is the ultimate aim of the field-trialler.

Spaniel Trials

In spaniel field trials there must be two judges. In the spaniel championship both judges must be on the A Panel. In the open stakes both must be panel judges, one of whom must be on the A Panel. In all other stakes at least one of the judges must be on the A Panel. Dogs are called into line for the first round: the odd numbers will go to the right-hand judge and even numbers to the left. In the second round it is vice versa. The judge will indicate to the handler the extent of his beat (the ground to be worked). The judges will be looking for a dog with a good ground treatment which uses the wind to his advantage, in fact, a good natural game-finder, a dog with plenty of pace and style. Only the dog with plenty of pace can cover the ground thoroughly with the gun walking at a comfortable pace. I have witnessed all too often at spaniel trials some handlers who consistently pull their dogs back to do the same bit of ground again and again. They either do not have any confidence in their dogs' ability or, I suspect, are a by-product of judges who assume that any game that gets up behind the line has been missed by the dog. These judges must be wiser men than I for when shooting over my own spaniels over the years I have witnessed countless times the dog move a rabbit or bird that did not present itself to be shot but doubled back behind the line. So judges must be absolutely sure that a dog has missed game before discarding it.

After a successful hunt, find, flush and shot a judge would expect the spaniel to, if possible, have marked the fall and retrieve on command without assistance from his handler, or to be handled if the dog was not in a position to mark. If ground game was shot the dog should follow the line from the point of flush to the kill.

A spaniel should at all times work within gun range with good treatment of ground and must not pass over game on the beat that he is working. A spaniel's first job is to find game and flush it within the range of the gun. The direction of the wind is a considerable influence on the way a dog will work the ground. With a head-on wind the dog should quarter the ground systematically left to right and vice versa making good all likely game-holding cover, but keeping within gunshot of the handler. With a following wind it would be very different, the dog would often want to pull well out and work back

John Halstead handling Garenden Pip at the Yorkshire Sporting Spaniel Field Trial, watched by the judge Rodney Berry (Courtesy of Mr R. Shaw)

towards the handler. Judges should regulate the pace of the line to allow the dog to do this and make good his ground. The dog should not be penalised for missing game when in fact the line has been moving forward too fast to permit him to make good the ground; lines and foot scents should be ignored. Persistent pulling on foot scent is annoying and unprofitable resulting in game being missed. A dog should have plenty of drive and face cover well. A dog should also stop to game and shot but if he moves in order to mark the fall, if this is obscured, it shows intelligence and should be credited. For instance, in thick cover a dog should push game into the open and then check after doing so.

After both judges have seen all the dogs they may want to run off several dogs to decide on their final placings. It is very important that a good patch of ground should be selected to compare one dog's ground treatment against another, with guns still shooting. All too often I have witnessed the run-off take place on ground that is totally devoid of cover, with a small dog running off against a larger dog and invariably under these circumstances the smaller dog wins the day.

I started this chapter with the words 'What is a field trial?' So now let us ask the question, 'What use are field trials and how do they benefit the ordinary shooting man, if at all?'

I quite often get enquiries for trained gundogs and very early on in the conversation the enquirer will state that he does not want a field-trial dog, shortly followed by a description of what I consider to be a field-trial dog! I know what most of them mean. They do not require their retrievers to handle at great distances or their spaniels to have as much drive as in field trials. I also hear statements like, 'You can't shoot over field-trial dogs, they are too hot.' Now this is nonsense, for I can honestly say that every trained dog, whether retriever, spaniel or pointer, that I have had could be passed on to the ordinary shooting man, for I shoot over all my dogs and if I could not shoot over a trial dog then I would be the first to say that something must be wrong. On the other hand there are quite a few dogs which gain some success in field trials which, in my opinion, are not properly trained but managed. By this I mean the handler is in almost constant touch with his dog by movements of his hands, hissing etc. So like everything else, buy from a reputable individual, someone with a reputation to maintain.

By far the best service that field trials do for the shooting man and the gundog breeds in general is that when you acquire a puppy with all field-trial bloodlines on both sides of the pedigree and more than a smattering of winners then it is the nearest you can get to quality control. For at least the pedigree is saying that most, if not all, of his ancestors have been tested under normal shooting conditions and have not portrayed any vices. At least you are assured that there won't be any skeletons in the cupboard.

The HPRs

GEOFF HARGREAVES

Although born and brought up in town, Geoff Hargreaves has always been a countryman at heart, escaping to the countryside whenever possible and surrounding himself with livestock and dogs at every opportunity. He owned his first dog at the age of seven, when an old man surreptitiously slipped him a terrier pup in a carrier bag when Christmas shopping with his mother in Woolworths. There then followed a series of dogs of 'mixed' ancestry, trained to the catapult and airgun and to his own requirements. It was not until 1971, when he acquired his first German shorthaired pointer, that he became involved in 'formal' dog training and handling. When this bitch, handled by Geoff's wife, Barbara, won a strong class in the first championship show in which he was entered, followed shortly afterwards by an easy win of the first working test that both Geoff and the dog had been involved with, there began a deep and consuming involvement with HPRs which continues to the present day.

Although run purely as a hobby, their Ghyllbeck kennel name is known throughout the HPR world and is synonymous with quality dogs of outstanding working ability. As well as GSPs, they have had Hungarian vizslas and spinones in their kennel but their greatest success has been in large munsterlanders – they have made up two full champions.

A Panel B field-trial judge, Geoff has also been approved by the Kennel Club to award challenge certificates to GSPs and large munsterlanders, as has his wife and they are both proud to have been founder members of the German Shorthaired Pointer Association.

A great admirer of the German gundog system, Geoff regularly visits Germany to attend trials and to meet breeders and has imported breeding stock from Germany to improve existing British munsterlanders.

In common with the rest of Europe, the British Isles has an ancient and deep-rooted sporting tradition which is evident in all kinds of aspects of day-to-day living. Examples may be found in art, literature, architecture and even modern language of how closely woven with the fabric of everyday life 'la chasse' used to be, far more closely than is generally realised and infinitely more so than is the case today. Consequently, considering the history of these islands, it is not surprising that the breeds of sporting dogs which originated in Britain and Ireland, as essential adjuncts to all types of venery, are known and appreciated throughout the world, wherever game is pursued. However, despite the renown of our sporting breeds, there is one noticeable omission.

Alone in Europe, the British Isles, though rich in famous gundog breeds, cannot lay claim to its own national breed of hunt, point, retriever. Why this should be so when practically every country on the Continent has developed its own and in several instances more than one breed of hunt, point, retriever is unclear. It may, in some part, be due to the fact that we in Britain have always tended to specialise and consequently have developed specialist breeds, hunting our deer with deerhounds and staghounds, our hares with harriers and beagles, our foxes with foxhounds and terriers and even our gundogs have been bred to concentrate on one aspect of the sport, setters and pointers to point the game, retrieving breeds to retrieve it and spaniels to do the bits in between.

Our continental counterpart, however, has developed his sport in a different way, following the path of the true hunter, pursuing his quarry on foot and relying on one breed of dog to help him to do this. In Germany especially, this combination of functions is not confined to dogs but is extended to include the hunter's weapons. For, although unknown here, multi-barrelled firearms which incorporate both large and small-bore rifles as well as shotguns in one weapon are very popular and an obvious advantage in the circumstances for which they are designed. In this way the German hunter is equipped to deal with whatever species he may encounter in completely natural conditions, be it red deer, wild boar or partridge and, not surprisingly, he expects his dog to be equally prepared. All of which serves to underline the difference between our methods and those used on the Continent.

On the other hand, France has several of its own hunt, point, retriever breeds in addition to being famous for numerous breeds of packhounds, including the well-known bassett, so that knocks the specialisation theory on the head. Whatever the reason, the fact remains that, to paraphrase Robert Burns, hunt, point retrievers are 'nane o' Britain's dogs'.

The foreign origin of these breeds is emphasised by the name under which they have been officially classified within the gundog group. Whereas the native breeds are recognised by descriptive, one-word titles – the pointers and setters do just that – because we do not have an indigenous hunt, point, retrieve breed of our own and consequently have had to 'invent' a family name, the continentals have been lumbered with the cumbersome mouthful of hunt, point, retrievers, a title which attempts to describe them by their function but which is invariably abbreviated to HPR. The German term for HPRs is *gebrauchshund* which translates, as closely as is possible, to 'utility dog', a term which is commonly used in America but one which always makes me think of ration books. I have long hoped for the inspiration to produce a slick, snappy, descriptive alternative but as yet, to no avail.

The German influence on the HPR group in Britain is quite apparent and is not surprising since Germany is rich in HPR breeds and the first of these breeds to be introduced here came from that country. However, with the growth of interest in HPRs and, no doubt, assisted by the increasing ease of travel and communication, we are seeing a steady increase in the number of breeds within the group, from various countries on the Continent and we shall probably continue to do so. It is generally accepted that HPRs were introduced into Britain by members of the armed forces who had seen and appreciated their prowess whilst serving in Germany immediately following World War II. It would appear to be simply a quirk of fate that German shorthaired pointers and weimaraners should have been the breeds which the military men encountered and introduced to Britain, as neither of these is any more popular with shooting men in their homeland than any of half a dozen other breeds. Whatever the reason, these two represented the vanguard for HPRs in Britain and ultimately established themselves as the mainstay for the group, where they remain to the present day.

For some time following their arrival here, HPRs made only slight progress and were very rarely seen on shoots being generally regarded as novelties. During these early years, these breeds acquired a somewhat unenviable reputation, being labelled with all kinds of accusations including unruliness and the possession of hard mouths. This was despite the fact that GSPs had soon demonstrated their value by establishing themselves as a force to be reckoned with in the field-trialling world, winning awards at all levels. Moreover, this success was achieved in setter and pointer trials, since GSPs, being newcomers, had, at that time, no organisation structured for their requirements.

Exactly what proportion of these derogatory allegations could be substantiated and what had more basis in bias is open to speculation but there are numerous factors which could have been relevant. First of all, their 'newness' and 'foreign nature' would not have helped, as there is no counter-measure to good, old-fashioned prejudice. There was a great amount of hostility directed at the new breeds from the more blinkered members of the shooting fraternity in the early days on account of nothing more than their country of origin, but fortunately this attitude is now dying out along with its adherents. Commonsense dictates that the Germans, whose reputation for thoroughness and efficiency is legendary and who are accustomed to excellence, are not likely to accept less than the best in their dogs, particularly when the dogs

Brittany spaniel, a lesser-known member of the HPRs

Paley

German shorthaired pointer – 'a specialist but also a competent performer'

Flatcoat retriever – 'an extrovert but loyal servant'

The air scenters are seen at their best in open country

are to be used for a purpose which they take as seriously as they do their hunting. Of course, this does not mean that the HPRs are perfect paragons or 'all things to all men': that is not possible, they have their shortcomings just as do all breeds. I would not, for instance, expect one of these dogs to shine as a 'peg-dog' sitting still for drive after drive, just waiting to pick up, they are not designed for this type of work. Their trainers did, however, expect them to be capable of doing it if called upon and consequently they are tested on this capability in their homeland.

It is an odd characteristic of the gundog world, that should, for instance, a spaniel be observed to be hard-mouthed, he is regarded as simply a hard-mouthed spaniel, or if a retriever behaves in an unruly or noisy fashion, the dog is considered to be nothing more than a bad specimen. Whereas, if any of these faults is displayed by a dog belonging to the HPR group, this immediately condemns the entire breed out of hand in the eyes of the more biased critics. However, despite all this, HPRs continued to assert themselves as master craftsmen in the field and were rewarded in 1958 by the Kennel Club's inauguration of their own hunt, point, retriever group. Since the late seventies we have seen an upsurge in interest in HPRs and there is now a good number of dedicated handlers spread throughout all the breeds currently available, who appreciate their characteristics and who produce shooting dogs the equal of any in the country. There can now be few shoots in Britain where HPRs are unknown.

Why HPRs should have remained unknown here until such a relatively recent date is, to me, a mystery for it is inconceivable that hunters, travelling in pursuit of their sport, were unaware of the continental breeds of gundogs. The Victorians and Edwardians, in the heyday of organised shooting, were great travellers and collectors and considering the close relationship of all the royal houses of Europe, there must have been great to-ing and fro-ing throughout the Continent to sample all the specialities which each area had to offer, from the snipe-rich bogs in the west of Ireland to the legendary estates of Hungary, far to the east.

It is on record that Gordon setters were popular in Germany at the turn of the century and doubtless there were reciprocal arrangements with German breeds. If this did happen, records must have been lost or possibly destroyed on account of the tragic events during the first half of this century. It is known that German-owned shops and properties in this country were attacked by an irate populace at the outbreak of World War I, so it is possible that other items of German origin suffered similar treatment. There are accounts of individual dogs here and there in Britain at various times previous to the period in question and my good friend Major Clifford Fordyce-Burke has told me of GSPs at his family home near Stirling in the twenties. However, for all practical purposes the starting point for HPRs on this side of the Channel is generally regarded as the immediate post-war period.

This is not the case in America, where HPRs, particularly German shorthaired pointers and weimaraners have been popular for many decades, obviously having been originally taken there as the companions of German immigrants who maintained close links with their homeland and ensured the continuance of the breeds by the importation of thoroughbred blood. This tradition is still maintained in the United States where many of the breed clubs are administered by people of German extraction who ensure that the affairs of the breeds are conducted closely on German standards. This applies particularly to field trials, which means that HPRs are required to perform HPR functions to HPR standards thereby maintaining the working abilities of the breeds.

So, what is the attraction of these newcomers when there are so many established gundog breeds available in Britain? The first point in their favour must be their versatility. Every one of these dogs is equally at home amongst the grouse on a moor, ranging the stubbles for partridge, thrashing dense woodland for pheasant or rabbit or working the foreshore when the geese are in. Their relatively large size gives them the strength and stamina to quarter vast areas of ground for long periods and to cope easily with the largest hare or goose, whilst their agility ensures that stone walls and spate rivers offer slight obstruction. To have all this, plus the capability to produce

A German shorthaired pointer freezes to a strong scent

classic points, in one dog is a certain recipe for memorable shooting days.

The German Shorthaired Pointer

Without doubt, the German shorthaired pointer is the best known breed of the HPR group in Britain. It has been established here the longest and has proved itself to be not only a competent exponent of all gundog work but has an unequalled reputation as a family dog, guard and show dog par excellence.

During its thirty-five year history in Britain, the breed has produced a constant flow of champions of all types. Show champions, which indicates that the breed is as sound as the standard requires, full champions, which are champion dogs capable of doing their job, or in this case, usually proven working dogs which are sound enough to win in the show ring. Field trial champions are made up every season and this is despite the fact that there are at present only fifty HPR trials each year, a proportionately lower number of which are championship qualifiers. But most remarkable of all, the GSP regularly demonstrates that it is the only breed of the two dozen or so recognised by the Kennel Club, which is capable of producing dual champions, a feat which the breed manages to accomplish approximately every four years. There are those in the gundog world who, for reasons known only to themselves attempt to denigrate this achievement, even though the fact remains that, under Kennel Club rules, the qualifications are exactly the same for all gundog breeds, yet the GSP remains unique.

The GSP comes in three colours, arranged in a variety of ways which provide the following permitted combinations. Solid liver, when the dog is liver coloured all over; liver and white, which gives a wide variety of effects from almost solid liver, with a white flash on face, tail, chest or foot to almost entirely white with a liver head; and black, distributed in a similar manner to that described for the liver. The black colouration reputedly results from the introduction of black pointer blood in an attempt to improve pigmentation. GSPs with this colouration are much less common than their liver relations.

Although descending from the ancient German pointing breeds, the GSP, as we know it, did not appear till late last century and was not perfected until the twentieth. Nevertheless, the thoroughness of the work of the early pioneers can be observed from the reputation which the breed now enjoys.

The Weimaraner

Despite being rarely seen in the shooting field, the weimaraner is easily the numerically strongest breed in the HPR group. His striking appearance appeals not only to shooters but also to people who have no connection with the function for which the breed was developed. As a result, there are few weimaraners which are qualified in the field, although breed history has been made this very season by Mrs Di Arrowsmith and her dog Wobrook of Fleetapple, who has become the breed's first field-trial champion. Di

Weimaraner

Weimaraner puppy – an increasingly popular breed

has retired him now at the age of nine, with twenty-four trial awards and Brook bowed out by winning three successive open championship qualifiers, not a bad finale.

The weimaraner is distinguished in one particular field, that of working trials, where dogs are required to perform intricate tests of control, obedience, scenting and intelligence and has built a record as one of the most capable gundog breeds competing in this field. A number of weimaraners have gained top awards in working trials and one, Mr Bob Lynch's Ch Reeman Aruac, has qualified in the field as well as being a show champion and bearing the working-trial title CDex, UDex, WDex, TDex. I was pleased to be running in the trial where Bob won his field-trial award and remember him telling me of when he started training to the gun. Brig was already, at that time, a show champion and TDex but took to his gun training like the natural which he is. At some stage in his training, Bob had entered him in a working trial, during which he was performing his scent trail with his usual flair, when he suddenly swung into the wind and adopted a rigid point. On being invited by the judge, who must have been a shooter, to work it out, Brig flushed three grouse from a patch of heather. It didn't do much for his marks but it showed that he had found out what weimaraners are really for and that there was nothing wrong with his hunting instincts.

Weimaraners are often criticised for their involvement in working trials, even by people from within the HPR group, with the allegation that the tracking and trailing exercises involved somehow impair their air-scenting abilities. This is, of course, complete nonsense as the exercises are very similar to the blood-trailing tests which are a mandatory part of all HPR trials in Germany, moreover, as every huntsman knows, scent is where you find it and it is pointless a dog waving his nose about in the air if scent is sticking to the ground. Furthermore, it has long been accepted that tracking and trailing requires a more sensitive nose than does pointing, and obviously weimaraners have proved themselves adept at this skill. Always that distinctive steel-grey colour, whether in the normal short coat or the much rarer long-haired variation, the weimaraner is a most impressive and aloof dog with an ever-growing circle of admirers.

The Hungarian Vizsla

The Hungarian vizsla arrived in Britain at around the same time as the GSP and the weimaraner and yet has had only slow and gradual growth in popularity and is much less numerous than the other two breeds. Accordingly, he is still a rarity in the shooting field possibly on account of his temperament

German wirehaired pointer on point in stubble turnips

which requires slightly different training from 'normal' and which can, at times, be rather trying. Nevertheless, properly trained and handled, vizslas can make excellent shooting dogs, as has been demonstrated by husband and wife team, Nigel and Sylvia Cox who have an impressive trialling record and who, in fact, produced the breed's first and only field-trial champion to date FTCh Vizsony of Valotta.

Originating, as the name indicates, in Hungary, the vizsla has a very long recorded history stretching back to the twelfth century and beyond. Structurally similar to the previous two breeds, the vizsla is somewhat finer boned but his most distinctive feature is his rich, russet-gold coat, which makes him a real eye-catcher but not the dog to take on a fox drive.

The German Wirehaired Pointer

The next continental to arrive on the scene in Britain came, once again, from Germany in the form of the German wirehaired pointer. Although reputed to be the most popular hunter's dog in his homeland, the GWP made only a slow start here following his introduction but in recent years there has been a strong growth in the breed's popularity.

Similar in build and colour to the GSP, the GWP was nevertheless developed from two different breeds, the *stichel* and the *Pudel* pointer. He has a very harsh coat of medium length and sports what the Germans call, a strong beard. Normally reserved and aloof, the GWP has a reputation as a one-man dog with a mind of his own but when trained he makes a tireless shooting companion of the most versatile sort.

The Large Munsterlander

Officially making his debut in 1972, the next import was again from Germany and this time one with a long coat, the large munsterlander. Named after his area of origin in northern Germany, and also to identify him from his smaller cousin, this is the only breed in the group whose standard does not call for him to be docked, the operation being left optional, although working strains are usually docked by the customary ½in.

Although there are only a handful of qualified champions, the breed can boast a field trial champion in Clara of Abbotsbourne, owned, trained and handled by Mr John Wagstaff, a breed stalwart of long standing. The breed is not often seen in competition but is nevertheless appreciated by a growing number of shooters and keepers who value his enthusiasm and biddable nature. Always black and white, munsters can vary enormously in appearance from almost all white with a black head to almost solid black. A mottled roan blending of the two colours is known as *schimmel* in German, which translates as mildew, a very descriptive term.

The Brittany

France is the home of the next newcomer, as one would expect with a name like the Brittany and what a success story. For despite only having been here since 1982, the breed already has its first field trial champion, Riscoris Fleur de Lys which was successfully steered to her title by her owner Angela Lewis. This breed has attracted probably a greater proportion of shooting and trialling people in relation to its numbers than any other HPR breed, no doubt partly due to its resemblance to spaniels. But I suspect that the amount of care obviously taken to select the already large number of imports from proven strains in both France and America, where the breed is very popular, also has some influence.

However, the Brittany's behaviour in the field reveals that it is a definite HPR, fast, wide ranging and a staunch pointer. I have several times had the pleasure of judging these little dogs in trials and seen them take first place frequently in the face of competition from dogs of the better known breeds. It is possible that their apparent speed is an illusion since they are, at 20in to the shoulder, easily the smallest member of the group and are probably no faster than any other but they certainly are exciting to watch. They also present a greater variation in colour than any other HPR, as their standard allows black and white, liver and white, orange and white, roan and tri-colours. They also incidentally are occasionally born with a naturally docked tail.

The Spinone

The latest of these breeds to reach our shores hails from Italy and is known as the spinone. A large, impressive dog, the largest, in fact, in the group, spinones come in a variety of colours including all white, white and orange and white and brown in various combinations. Very calm in temperament, the spinone has a much slower working pace than other HPRs. Reputedly very popular in northern Italy amongst shooters, the spinone has yet to make his name here in the shooting field, although a few have been trialled. The spinone has a long history and several writers of Ancient Rome make reference to the dog in their works. The breed has, on the other hand, made an impact here in the show ring and is growing strongly in numbers; it is to be hoped that this does not prove detrimental.

That is a brief run down on all the HPR breeds currently recognised here in Britain. But it is by no means the end of the story, for, as previously mentioned, most countries of Europe have their own HPR, the majority of which are still unknown here. The braques of France, the drentses of Holland and many more from Germany, to mention but a few, present an exciting prospect for the shooter and dog man who admires the unusual and no doubt some of these breeds will find their way here with time.

Training

The first thing to remember when starting to train your first HPR is, forget about the other breeds. That is to say, do not attempt to impose on them the same methods which would apply to a spaniel or retriever. They must learn discipline and basic obedience just the same as any other breed but there are a number of differences which must be remembered if the dog is not to be inhibited.

For someone who has always been used to dogs working around his feet, the sight of a dog performing its task 100–200yd away is quite horrifying, but that is what these dogs are meant to do, to range far and wide in quest of game. The difference is that when they find their quarry, they do not just bustle into it and hope that the gun is within shot, they hold the game and wait to present it for the gun. Of course, on a well-stocked moor, for instance, where there may not be the need to cover as large an area to find game, they will adjust their beat accordingly. Similarly, in heavier cover, it is of little benefit for the dog to be working where he is obscured from view, so once again, he will cover his ground to suit. The point is that HPRs must be capable of covering ground when required and a dog which has been restrained from putting distance between himself and his handler will be reluctant or afraid to do so when asked. Of course, this free-running approach does not mean that they should be allowed to run riot; just remember that you can control drive and enthusiasm but you cannot put it in if it is not there.

Then you are going to have to learn to wait. Whilst it is perfectly possible to have a retriever trained at twelve months old, there is no way that this can be done with an HPR. For a start, they have three times as many skills to perfect in addition to being slow developers. I always reckon on three years before a dog is a competent, fully trained worker. Admittedly, as in any other field, there are exceptions. I had a munster which was trialling at eighteen months old and in her first season took an award at all five trials entered. But as a rule, I prefer the slow starters, they seem to end up the best. A GSP bitch which I had was completely unruly up to the age of two. I could scarcely do a thing with her apart from 'sit' and recall (sometimes). She did, however, show all the right signs so I decided to wait. Gradually the penny dropped and she quickly developed into a useful gundog, winning several field trial awards including first, but more importantly she made an honest, dependable worker.

It is most important for one of these dogs to have a stress-free puppyhood lasting as long as the puppy needs. As with all breeds, individuals develop at different rates and some puppies are ready for the introduction of different exercises earlier than others but certainly to attempt to start a lesson which a

Pointer under firm control

puppy cannot easily perform is asking for trouble. There is no set time-scale, the puppy will tell you when he is ready.

The innate intelligence of these breeds is another important factor to consider when training. Expecting an HPR to mindlessly chase dummies all day or to vigorously work a bowling green is to invite certain disappointment, they are too intelligent for that. Once a puppy has demonstrated that he is a willing retriever it is pointless to keep throwing dummies day after day and can be counter-productive. Many HPRs, and in particular munsters, dislike contrived situations and quickly become bored and unco-operative and to insist on continuance is to court disaster. On the other hand, there are individuals for whom it is not possible to throw sufficient dummies and if you find that you happen to have one of these dogs, you can have a lot of fun at working tests, if that is your wont. But remember, you can't make a dog enjoy chasing dummies.

The high level of intelligence which these dogs possess enables them to learn quickly and they are soon ready for the next step. So it is important to recognise when an exercise has been absorbed and to avoid constant repetition in an effort to achieve perfection. Just occasional practice is the secret. Incidentally, their brainpower also means that they can quickly sense which party is winning in a battle of wills, so stubbornness and obstinacy must be distinguished from confusion or misunderstanding. Of course, with an advanced dog it is possible to perform all kinds of feats of distance control and 'circus tricks' but this can often be at the expense of the dog's natural ability and initiative and I personally find that I derive far more pleasure from working with dogs whose natural skills have been developed to their peak. I have repeatedly found that HPRs improve with experience and I frequently find that a young dog which has surprised me with his ability one season goes on to amaze me in the next.

In spite of being in possession of great levels of energy, HPRs are usually economical with it when they are experienced. For instance, don't expect them to barge into every patch of dense cover in search of imaginary game. They rely on their senses to tell them if game is present under brambles and the like and if they think the effort is worthwhile, they will do a fair impression of a white rhino, but if there is no game present 'what's the point?' is their attitude. Similarly, they quickly get bored with barren ground and a beat which offers no indication of game quickly reduces them to a remarkable level of lethargy demonstrated by leg-cocking, muck rolling and the like. All of these characteristics must be borne in mind when beginning to train one of the HPR breeds, particularly for the first time, and especially when graduating from one of the more conventional breeds.

It is also important to recognise that although all these breeds are classified together because of their manner of working, they each have their own subtle, and in some cases not so subtle, differences and it is wrong to expect one particular breed to perform exactly as another breed does. There are those within the HPR group who fail to recognise these differences, using their own favourite breed as a yard-stick and criticising other breeds which don't meet these imagined standards. This attitude is completely incorrect as each one of these breeds was developed to meet the standards and objectives of its pioneers and though they all perform the same function, they each do it in their own way with one no more 'correct' than the other. By the same token, all HPR breeds in Germany are tested to a common standard under a common set of rules in order to qualify as a recognised working dog.

If you do decide to try one of these 'foreigners', remember the basic steps. First of all choose your breed and this is really only a matter of personal preference. Having done that, find out what you can about it, its background, its characteristics, its requirements and which kennels are producing the *proven* workers. Then pick your pup and having got him home, *take your time*. If you go about it in the correct way, it will be a decision which you will never regret and I guarantee that the dog will teach you far more than you will ever teach him.

Kenzie

JOHN HUMPHREYS

I named him after the great Mackenzie Thorpe, the famous Wash wildfowler and goose man, an extrovert character as well as a remarkable shooting man. Kenzie lived up to the name for of all forms of shooting; it was probably as a wildfowling dog that he excelled. He was well bred being a grandson of the great Sandringham Sidney, owned by Her Majesty the Queen and trained by Bill Meldrum, the Sandringham head keeper and dog man who has contributed a chapter to this book.

He was another in the line of large, tough, black, dog labradors I was to own and, although I never intended it to be that way, those were the dogs which inevitably seemed to come my way. I spent more time on his training than I had on any of my other dogs and yet he was the most badly behaved. I came to the conclusion that, although his looks were classical, he had grace and power, a boldness and nose which I have rarely seen equalled, he was not very intelligent. Religiously, every single day from puppyhood, I took him on his footpath walk, keeping him to heel, teaching him to sit, encouraging him to work and trying him with a few dummies – much as you would do with any new dog.

I came to the reluctant conclusion that he was not going to be a success, for he just did not seem to learn a single thing. Even when he was ten years of age he would not sit unless you pushed his rump firmly downwards, a lesson mastered by many puppies a few weeks old. Walking to heel seemed to be quite beyond him. I tried chain leads, chokers, a whippy stick but all to no avail. In desperation I investigated the American electric collar, a device whereby you could give a dog a sharp electric shock at some range if he was being headstrong. Friends warned against it but it was only because I could not get hold of one that I did not try it. I sent him to a local trainer, a giant of a man who would surely be able to dominate him, but he had to send him back after two days and confess himself bested. He was breaking my heart in those early years and at one point I was so desperate that I considered offering him as a free gift to a good home.

On a shooting day he would not stay at my peg but stood, his tail thrashing against my legs, running-in to everything, stealing the birds of neighbours, creeping away from me when he thought I was not looking and generally proving an over-large handful. I tried a giant corkscrew of the sort you see advertised to tether uncertain dogs, but there was no ground firm enough to hold him. I could not, with all my strength pull the thing out of the ground but he could and did so frequently. On top of that was the nuisance of carrying that muddy piece of metal and the palaver of screwing it into the ground at every stand. I took to tying him to a stout tree or fence post when there was one handy. The latter he could often pull out of the ground and I have known him bite through the length of cart rope which did duty as a lead and make good his escape.

Five thousand times I called him to heel, five thousand times he refused. Five thousand times I told him to sit and it was not until I had added a hefty clout to the command that he would reluctantly comply, giving me a hurt expression as though I was asking something entirely new and unreasonable of him. In a hide he was a liability. It was absurd that I would take pains to conceal myself on a salting, crouching in a tiny creek below a narrow fringe of spartina or sit on the bank of a fen dyke waiting for mallard while he would sit up on top like the figurehead of a Viking ship visible to duck miles away. It was a real struggle and a wrestling match to get him below eye level. When there he would spend the evening inching his way back up to his old position, shifting a tiny distance each time my back was turned when we would have to go through the traumatic process again.

You may well be asking yourself why I should have bothered at all to have taken him; surely he would have been better at home where he could not annoy me. Firstly, it has to be a very bad dog who is worse than no dog at all, and I tended to be a one-dog man and had to live with my decisions for the lifespan of the animal in question. I was no high-powered dog man with full kennels to chop and change and get rid of anything less than FTCh potential. The second and more telling point was that Kenzie was, for all his faults, an amazing retriever. No distance was too great for him, no swim too far and he had an extraordinary nose. He was working for himself, mind you, and not for me, but once on a line of a running pheasant there was no stopping him.

Pheasants in the Fens, wild birds especially, can run for three or four fields, for there are not the friendly bramble patches of more comfortable covert shoots into which runners go to ground and where any picker-up worth the name will concentrate his efforts. Our pheasants run across ditches, down rows of sugar-beet in 40acre fields, over corn drills and away. Kenzie has been known to vanish from sight on such occasions and it was not often that he came back empty mouthed. Once my young son took him rough shooting and at his first shot the boy hit a pheasant which came tumbling down apparently mortally wounded. Kenzie set off to the fall, overran it and kept going until he was a black speck in the distance. Peter yelled and whistled, half-thinking that he had lost the dog and also believing that the bird was lying close to the fall. In fact it had got up and run like a redshank in thick cover and the dog actually crossed the parish boundary into the next village before he caught up with it and came pounding back.

Once I saw him chase a strong running red-legged partridge which had enough steam left in it to fly across one of our steep-banked dykes. Kenzie took off, snatched the bird in mid-air with an audible clop of his jaws and plummeted down 10ft to the water below which he hit with an awesome splash and eruption of muddy weed. Once he retrieved a fox which had been shot, a large dog, which he carried back 80yd completely clear of the ground. He was very strong.

I took him grouse shooting to a little moor in Yorkshsire where I had a few days every season. He gave the Swaledale sheep a hard time, retrieved many spectacular grouse but nearly broke my arm and my heart into the bargain. His failure to walk at heel and the fact that grouse are up and away quickly enough not to need any flushing meant that I had to keep him on the lead at all times. How he pulled! I tied the rope lead round my shoulders, one end tied to my belt, and one held in my hand. It was hard enough to walk those uneven miles of peat hags and broken ground without any impediment and at the end of the day I was exhausted and my hands were blistered and raw from where I had been continually hauling him back.

However, like Cassius of ill-fated memory, the cry would go up to 'Fetch Kenzie!' if there was any especially hard bird or one which had beaten the other dogs. My mental and physical agonies were worthwhile when, as he did more than once, he wiped the eyes of the beautifully trained, knee-hugging dogs of my fellow sportsmen. Once we were all hunting for a dropper in one patch of heather and as usual, Kenzie wandered off on business of his own; savagely I watched him go knowing that, as usual, he would be deaf to the whistle. My feelings changed rapidly when, five minutes later, he came back with the bird and an expression which said, 'Piece of cake!'

It was as a wildfowling dog that he excelled. I had the shooting on a pond hidden in some wild country in the Fens and the mallard would pour into it on winter nights, especially when I had scattered a little tail barley in the shallows. I evolved a custom of taking three guests to shoot and Kenzie and I would do the picking-up. It was not often that he lost a bird, plunging his head underwater for the divers, working far over the bank in the dark in the jungle beyond for a bird which had slanted off wounded, and remembering where others had fallen. When a pack of birds came in at once and the shooting was fast and furious, he might have as many as five birds to pick in one operation. At times he brought back two at once. There were many nights when he alone had retrieved a score of duck.

His rheumatics grew painful in later life and I took to giving him 'Bute' in pill form when he was in for a heavy day. His enormous workload made him hard on himself for he was constantly working and at the age of nine when many dogs still have a lot left in them, he looked an aged pensioner. I had to lift him into the truck for the homeward journey, although he seemed always able to struggle up when he felt an expedition was afoot and he was in danger of missing something.

In later life he developed a new vice, strange, for I felt that there were none left *for him to adopt. He chewed things in the back of the truck after a hard day. Bill Meldrum mentions this syndrome elsewhere in this book and gives as the reason overtiredness after continual exertion. Such may be the case but it was cold comfort to find the picnic basket demolished and once the shoot photograph album almost completely eaten. If there was any trouble going, Kenzie would be into it.*

As I write he is still going strong. I shall withdraw him from the formal shooting field next season and keep him for occasional pigeon outings or duck shooting where he is most happy. He was quite simply too much of a handful on driven shoots, ruining my concentration, irritating other dogs and demanding my constant attention. As a picker-up he would have been superb, but during his lifetime I had rather dropped out of that scene and so he had no opportunity to prove the point.

He is an extrovert, a hooligan, a well-known character, a handful, and a trouble-maker, but he picked some of the best birds I have ever seen retrieved so I must forgive him his many vices. His sins are those of commission not of omission; he likes to be noticed and for the decade he shared with me and my gun, he provided many experiences, good and bad, which I will never forget.

Breeding

LOUISE PETRIE-HAY

Louise Petrie-Hay has owned dogs all her life. Since 1960, when her husband retired from the army and they bought a small farm in Worcestershire, she has specialised in breeding, training and working gundogs. Her Waidman prefix has been responsible for many winning GSPs, weimaraners and vizslas. After a short period in the show ring when she made up a GSP champion and a weimaraner champion, winning best of breed with both of them at Crufts, she concentrated on the working aspect of the dogs. Waidman Brok is the sire of the first vizsla field-trial champion and is in the pedigrees of most of the field-trial winning vizslas today. She is a Kennel Club Panel A field-trial judge for the HPR breeds, had the honour of judging their first championship stake and has represented them on the Kennel Club field trial committee for many years. She was field-trial secretary for the German Shorthaired Pointer Club for eight years and now as FT secretary for the Hungarian Vizsla Society has been responsible for promoting and encouraging this breed actively in the field. Her articles in the Shooting Times *and* Shooting Life *are always entertaining and informative, as is her recently published book* Gundogs, their History, Breeding and Training *published by Sporting Press.*

General

With the increase of so many pedigree breeds of dogs over the last century, dog breeding has become a commercial enterprise. Where cash is involved integrity often goes out of the window. Show champions and trained gundogs can demand big money. The inevitable result has been a split in many of the breeds – dogs bred purely for work and those bred for success in the show ring. A few altruistic breeders attempt to succeed in both worlds claiming that their

working gundogs can win not only field trials but also beauty competitions. This results in a dog which is commonly, but inaccurately, titled a dual champion. In fact the correct title is champion and field-trial champion. In the early part of this century this was not unusual because it was accepted that gundogs were bred for work and the show ring was merely proof that their conformation fitted the standard necessary for the animal to carry out its task in the field.

As time went by the standards were affected by fashion and the connection with working ability was forgotten. Naturally, those breeding for that ability lost their confidence in the show results and stopped entering their dogs. An inevitable rift became obvious so that today when considering the breeding of 'working' gundogs it is necessary to stress the importance of proven working ability in the pedigrees.

A breeder who owns two or more brood bitches has to have a licence from the local council. This was introduced in order, in some measure, to control the indiscriminate breeding of dogs. A licence is only issued after the conditions under which the bitches are kept and whelped have been inspected and approved by the local authority. It is doubtful in some cases whether this authority is aware of the rudimentary requirements for the hygienic and satisfactory breeding of puppies. In any case it has the effect that only those breeders who are likely to breed carefully will apply, whereas the backyard breeder is perfectly able to continue producing puppies for sale under appalling conditions, as are the puppy farmers whose arrangements are quite impossible to check unless reported once in a while by some conscientious citizen. The same situation arose with the dog licences, only those interested in the welfare of their dogs bought them, leaving as many if not more dogs unlicensed. If those buying puppies could be persuaded to buy only from licenced breeders, much could be done to eliminate a lot of the suffering of bitches which are bred from at every heat and puppies which are sent off in bulk to puppy farms where they are sold to anyone who has the cash to pay for them.

So when writing about breeding dogs it is just as important to consider the selling and buying of them. These three factors are entwined and cannot be divorced from each other. Each of them needs equal care and thought and if neglected can result in more dogs being dumped on the scrap heap of rescue kennels or the point of a hypodermic needle – and what an appalling waste that is.

If a dog is to hunt, point or to retrieve or to do all three jobs then he must have the right blood and be built in the right manner so that legs, muscles, heart and head work in unison to keep him fit, healthy and working happily for his allotted span of life. Don't consider bringing into the world puppies which are unable to achieve this either because they are poorly conformed, suffer from hereditary defects or lack essential good feeding when young to make adequate bone and muscle. The true interests of the gundog breeds would be served by having breed masters such as the Germans have but this would hardly be acceptable to the Englishman. However a lot more could be contributed to thoughtful breeding by the breed societies if their rules included the exclusion of membership where a breeder was known to be breeding and selling defective stock. A hereditary defect in setters was eliminated by controlled breeding advised by that society. The Weimaraner Club, in its early days, took a firm hand in seeing that the interests of the breed were guarded. Recently the English Gordon Setter Club proposed to request that the Kennel Club refuse to register any Gordon setter whose dam and sire had not been scored under the BVA KC Hip Dysplasia Scheme, and that this be incorporated into their own club rules.

It is natural that you should think of your own dog as a paragon of virtue and therefore suitable for breeding. I allow myself to admit that perhaps my dogs may have one or two small imperfections but if anyone agrees with me I feel the smile on my face edging away and a nasty steely glint coming into my eye while I mentally register them as permanent and unforgivable enemies. A sideline on the breeding scene are dogs or bitches sold on 'breeding terms'. This means that the owner relinquishes the right to use the dog for breeding. The breeder retains this right and dictates certain conditions which can be ratified by the Kennel Club. These conditions can vary enormously. The breeder can arrange to have the bitch back when it is time to have a litter, or the owner can breed a litter on the advice of the breeder and then hand over some or all the puppies of one or a number of litters. The breeder can also reserve the use of a stud dog, the owner being merely the keeper of the dog. These arrangements must suit some people as it is a fairly common practice among many breeds but not, I think, gundogs. If embarked upon it is essential that the agreement is carefully drafted to avoid any trouble which would ultimately cause distress to the dog involved.

Pros and Cons

The breeding of gundogs is probably the least stressful of all the breeds, primarily because the dogs bred from are fit, healthy and suited for an active and fruitful life. The chances are that the mating will be natural and the birth normal. However there can be exceptions and this is desperately worrying for the first-time breeder. The majority of puppies on the market are produced by professional breeders who have regular litters and experience in rearing them.

Many gundog-owners would like to have just one litter from their bitch or perhaps just one puppy sired by their dog. There are lots of reasons for this but the most common is that the dog pleases them and they realise that after ten or fifteen years this will end and a replacement must be found. What better than a son or daughter? Puppies are fun to rear and if there are children then it is good for them to realise that animals need very special and constant care and attention especially when young. It also involves quite a lot of work, not so much for the first four weeks when the pups are suckling,

Summer puppies can get out into the sunshine early

but after that when they need four meals a day at least, the attendant cleaning and the possible worries of a sick puppy. Regular attention is vital and other engagements have to be deferred quite often if the puppies are to be cared for properly.

Others just want the enjoyment of having puppies, and why shouldn't they? There is no reason why not, providing they remember that there will be anything from five to twelve puppies, and that they carry the responsibility of finding homes for those little dogs. Not just any homes, but the right homes. Although some may leave home fairly soon, say at eight weeks old, it is possible that some may remain for at least six months before the right owner comes along. Can they be properly accommodated, fed and exercised?

Others imagine that they might make a few quid. Some idiots think they will make more than a few quid. The cost of rearing a litter includes the mating fee, vet's bills, heating, special puppy food, extra meat for the bitch, innoculations, Kennel Club registration, supplements, medicines and the cost of running-on the pups that are not sold. If the money brought in by the sale of the litter covers these expenses and the cost of feeding the bitch for the next year, you will be lucky. I would not call that making money, particularly if you include the possible sleepless nights and worry if things go wrong.

Others believe that a bitch should have at least one litter for the good of her health, or that a stud dog is not fulfilled until his sexual appetite is satisfied. At one time the veterinary profession encouraged this belief but today they seem to advocate the reverse. Instead of waiting for a bitch to mature to about eighteen months before she can be spayed it is now possible to operate before her first season. Castration seems to be their answer to any abnormal behaviour in dogs. I have a strange hang-up on the subject of castration. I can accept that in the horse-world geldings are perfectly normal and acceptable, but to do the same operation to a male dog, unless there is an absolute necessity, such as cancer, is in my opinion a mutilation of the animal. When my husband and I returned from Germany we bought a GSP bitch. By the time she was eighteen months old we were going berserk because of her hyper-energy. There was nothing wrong with her other than a vast and insatiable appetite for work. This was hard to satisfy, so on the advice of our vet, we mated her because it 'should quieten her down'. Maybe it should have, but it did not. After three weeks of nursing her seven puppies she threw her maternal duties aside and insisted on reverting to her career-girl image, if anything, with more force than before. We were possibly unlucky as I believe, in some cases, a restless bitch can be calmed by breeding a litter.

Accidents can happen even in the most respectable families and rather than produce unwanted puppies it is advisable to have the bitch injected within twenty-four hours of the mating. If the misalliance has occurred in secret and the pregnancy is noticed only when it is too late to abort, then keep one or two pups rather than destroying them all. In this way the bitch can

This is no good for figure control!

express her maternal instincts and there is no risk of upsetting her hormone balance or her mental stability.

Selection of Breeding Stock

Breeding dogs involves a number of considerations. Breeding gundogs includes many more than the normal family pet. Working ability is a priority and includes correct conformation, quality of nose and softness of mouth. Temperament is just as important. Biting and fighting gundogs are no help to a shooting man. Lack of hereditary defects is essential and can be avoided with knowledge.

Hip Dysplasia is probably the commonest and can be the most crippling of the inherited defects. Some breeds suffer more than others. The result is lameness which is caused when the ball and socket joints of the hip do not fit correctly. It is a highly inherited polygenic characteristic. The British Veterinary Association Kennel Club scheme consists of a veterinary surgeon X-raying the hips and then submitting these X-rays to the panel who will allot a score for each hip. The lower the scores the sounder the hips will be. The *Kennel Club Gazette* publishes a monthly list of dogs which have been certified as 'Examined radiographically and certified under the KC/BVA scheme'. A dog must be over one year old before this is possible. It is obviously important before mating to be sure that the sire and dam do not have HD. For a stud dog which is used extensively then the score of his progeny is a better guide to the stud dog's breeding merit even than his own score. Some breed societies keep such a record, eg labradors and goldens. Most of the dogs for which X-rays are submitted for examination come from parents who have not gone through the scheme. If a dog suffers from HD the effects vary from considerable pain and immobility leading to inevitable destruction or, if only moderate, then to the inactive life of a family pet.

The Kennel Club also runs a veterinary scheme to cover inherited eye defects such as hereditary cataract and retinal dysplasia which affect gundog breeds. Ectropian and entropian eyelids are also hereditary eye defects. Congenital deafness, epilepsy in all its forms and diabetes can affect gundogs. This makes it very plain that only dogs which do not suffer from any of these faults should be used for breeding. In any intended mating honesty and integrity must be absolute when investigating the history of any defects in the pedigree.

Finally and equally important are outward appearance and expression. This must be pleasing if you are going to live with the dog. Beauty is in the eye of the beholder but an initial effort to breed a handsome pup goes a long way. We all like a pretty girl or a good-looking man but how this is ever achieved with the haphazard breeding that goes on among humans is beyond comprehension. With dogs at least we can select our breeding stock.

We can also arrange the time of year that is most suitable for the rearing of pups. Gundog people obviously prefer that their bitches are not tied up with a family during the shooting season, so summer puppies are chosen. For many reasons this is easier; perhaps no heating will be needed, the pups can get out in the sunshine at an early age and there is a lot less dirt if little feet are not wet and muddy. There again anyone who has ambitions in the field-trial world needs a pup born on or soon after 1 January as he will then remain classified as a puppy until he is nearly two years old. Pups qualify for puppy stakes and trophies if they are born after 1 January of the previous year of the trial, so a December pup will only be an official puppy for thirteen months of his life.

Decisions will have to be made as to whether to in-breed, line-breed or out-cross. To mate two dogs just because they are neighbours or because they belong to friends is foolish. Pedigrees are important because they will tell you how the dogs are related, if at all. In-breeding means close relationship, ie father and daughter, mother and son, brother and sister. In other words incest. Now incest is all right in dogs providing you know what you are doing. The effect will be that good and bad qualities will be exaggerated, as will the unknown. Breeders indulge in in-breeding if they want to tie a certain quality either in looks or ability. It often results in one 'flyer', some medium quality and some rubbish. This, of course, will not be evident until the pups are mature. Out-crossing is where two unrelated dogs are mated. The resulting progeny's abilities will be unknown as, although the qualities of both parents are acceptable, the resulting mixture will be unpredictable. Line-breeding is between the two. Dogs can be related but not closely, a bitch can be mated to her mother's brother's son. In this case the bitch's sire can be unrelated as can the brother's son's dam. There can be many variations to this type of mating resulting in the qualities of the related dogs being strengthened and passed down to the pups.

Any animal used for breeding must be fit, healthy, well fed and happy. The registration of any breeding stock should be checked with the Kennel Club if you wish to breed pedigree dogs. A lot of problems can occur later if one of the parents is not registered. It is possible to get the animal registered with the permission of the breeder providing that both the parents were registered, but this takes time and it is better to have this quite clear before the mating. Check also that all innoculations of both dog and bitch are up to date.

Mating

For a planned marriage of two dogs the normal procedure is for the bitch to visit the dog. There could be a number of reasons for this, some say that a dog is less likely to leave home looking for bitches if he can rely on them coming to him, also some sensitive dogs may not want to perform nuptial duties in strange surroundings. I can see both these arguments back-firing; a bitch in

A good enclosure is essential for lively puppies

season is just as likely to go in search of sex as is a dog, and she is just as easily upset by strange situations at mating time. However the dog gets preferential treatment and stays at home. It is also normal, having decided on a stud fee, to pay this after the service regardless of the result. If the dog has been proven, ie has sired previous litters, then the decision to pay cash or give the owner the choice of the litter must be clearly agreed, better still put in writing. If there are no puppies then it is possible that the dog's owner will agree to a second free mating but he is under no obligation to do so providing the dog is proven.

If a puppy is decided on in lieu of a fee and there should not be one of the chosen sex, then an alternative agreement should be reached. Once the litter is born and there is a queue of potential buyers on the doorstep it is very tempting to forget arrangements made with the stud-dog owner. A set date for selection should also be agreed so that other prospective buyers can then make their choice. Clear all this up before the mating. In the case of a mating where both dog and bitch are maidens, ie virgins, the owner of the bitch is taking a chance on using a dog which could be impotent or infertile. The dog has the advantage that a practice run will prove his ability, or lack of it, to father puppies. Equally there could be no pups because the bitch is barren. So it's a gamble and must be accepted as such. If a litter results then the owner of the bitch will be satisfied and should there be more than two or three pups will probably offer one to the stud-dog owner either to keep or sell. The owner of the stud dog will be satisfied because he now knows his dog is capable of producing pups so can charge for his services in future. Experienced breeders overcome this by proving their maiden stock with their own dogs.

Normally a bitch comes into season every six months but this can be variable. Weather can make a difference, a spring heat can be late should there be a very long cold winter; this is Nature's way of ensuring that the pups are not born in extreme conditions. The heat will last twenty-one days as a rule. Sometimes a young bitch's first heat can take a month before she is clear, but after that three weeks is average. The optimum time for mating is when the eggs have descended and are ready to be fertilised between the tenth and fourteenth day. When this happens the bitch will 'stand' for a dog, ie turn her tail sideways so that he can penetrate her easily. The exact time that a bitch is ready to be mated can vary as can the length of time she is prepared to accept a dog. This may last only a number of hours or a few days. A bitch will usually turn and snap at a dog if it is too early or too late. Alternatively, she may go on a sit-down strike. Stud dogs vary in their approach. Some like a friendly introduction and a romp before getting down to business, some prefer to be left alone with the bitch, some will let you handle or help them if things prove difficult and others are plain rapists. It is wiser not to leave the dogs together unsupervised unless they are both experienced and known to be sensible. A maiden bitch can do physical and mental damage to a stud dog by attacking him whilst he is mounting her or dragging him around once they are tied. This

can easily inhibit him in any further matings. A rough stud dog if left alone with a maiden bitch can frighten and damage her so that no pups will result and no further matings will be possible other than by forced matings.

Forced matings occur when the bitch is unwilling and has to be muzzled and held whilst the dog serves her. My only experience of this was when a bitch of mine was taken to a dog and was force-mated. The result was two dead puppies. The mating of two dogs should surely be a natural occurrence and if it is not I feel that probably Nature knows best. The 'tie' is rather boring. It is the time spent after the dog has penetrated the bitch and ejaculated, when his sexual organ expands so that it cannot be withdrawn until it retracts. This ensures that the sperm has time to sort itself out and find some eggs to fertilise. Having mounted the bitch the dog will bring one leg over her back and stand tail to tail. They will remain like this for anything from ten to forty minutes. At this time someone should be on hand in case they get restless so they can be quietened and restrained from pulling each other. You will appreciate that, if possible, it is sensible to organise a mating under cover should the weather turn sour. A cigarette and a cup of tea is an added refreshment if it is likely to be a long session. Once the dog has withdrawn then he should be given time to clean and tidy up and if possible the bitch should be prevented from urinating for an hour or so after. Everyone likes to know that a 'tie' has taken place as proof of the mating but it is possible for a bitch to conceive without one. Some bitches are too slack to hold the dog and provided he has ejaculated inside her then she could be fertilised.

If after a normal mating the bitch fails to whelp then a thorough veterinary check is advisable before another mating. A bitch can be infertile if her ovaries and womb are not fully developed. This could be caused by a hereditary defect in hormone production or acquired following damage to the central nervous system such as a head injury. Her oestrus cycle will be affected but this can sometimes be treated successfully with injections. Nymphomania is a condition where not only the heat is prolonged but recurs at short intervals. This is usually caused by cysts on the ovaries or by misuse of an oestrogen hormone. Injections or an operation can remove the cysts but they may recur. A major cause of acquired infertility is hypothyroidism, which is a decreased activity of the thyroid gland and in this case the bitch only comes into season once every two or three years or else has a very short heat at irregular times. This can be overcome by supplementing her thyroid secretion and restoring the reproductive organs to normal activity.

Whelping

The gestation period is sixty-three days, but this can vary up to a week either way. During this period the bitch should be treated normally. At about five weeks her nipples may become pink and begin to swell as will her tummy. Once these signs are apparent excessive exercise is best avoided as well as jumping. The proportion of her diet will have to be altered so that there is more protein and less carbohydrate. She should be dosed for roundworm

A hinged whelping box

at least three times during the pregnancy. Despite this the pups will have some worms but will not be born with infestation, which can, in severe cases, cause death.

Whether the pups are to be born in the house or an outbuilding is a matter for careful consideration but ensure that heat is available if necessary. Construct a suitable whelping box which should be big enough for her to lie down flat on her side and also to leave room for the pups to move around her. It is a good idea to have one side of the box hinged so that, once the pups are tottering about, the side can be lowered to allow them to stagger down the ramp and go exploring. Bedding material during labour must be disposable as it will get very soiled. Either shredded paper or old sheeting is ideal, not straw or shavings. No matter how tidily you arrange the nest the bitch will have ideas of her own and it is best to leave her to her own devices. Once the babies are born you can clean things up and give her fresh bedding which can be laundered and changed regularly.

Make her sleep and eat where she will whelp at least a week before the pups are due so that she accepts the situation and is happy and relaxed. Peace, quiet and darkness is what she will need once she begins her labour. An indication that her time is near is that she will become restless and start puffing and panting. She could behave like this for a few hours or a day or so before. Providing she is not in discomfort then let her alone and in due course the puppies will begin to arrive.

Should there be an interval of more than two hours between births then it would be wise to call the vet as it is possible that there could be a dead pup or a breach. Even maiden bitches seem to know how to cope with biting the umbilical cord, eating the afterbirth, drying the pups and encouraging them to start suckling. All you need to do is pay her a quiet visit from time to time to make sure that all is well and perhaps take her some warm, milky tea with glucose. Once they are all born she will want to nurse them and have a good sleep, no food is necessary as the afterbirths will sustain her for twenty-four hours at least, but make sure she has water. Leave her to recover in peace and quiet.

On the following day ask the vet to come and check that all is well with the bitch and check the puppies, you can then make arrangements for him to dock the tails and remove dew claws if this is necessary. If there are more pups than teats then take his advice as to whether she is capable of feeding the surplus or if you should help her by supplementing or acquiring the services of a foster mother. If any of the pups are deformed or poorly developed now is the time to ask the vet to destroy them. Again if there are more than you can be sure of placing in good homes then it is far kinder to kill them now than allow them to undergo the misery of being unwanted. Don't take on bottle feeding unless you are really dedicated. It can be quite exhausting persuading tiny puppies to accept a bottle every two hours day and night for two or three weeks.

Whilst the bitch is feeding her puppies she will need good food, plenty of fresh water, some exercise and extra vitamins and minerals. Her bed should be changed twice daily. The pups' eyes will start opening when they are about ten days old and a little later their ears will develop. From then on playtime is irresistible and is a fearful timewaster, but, in fact, this is a misnomer for the more the pups are gently handled the better they will be. Their individual characters and their confidence and affection for humanity begin to develop. If you have not the time then employ someone else as this is absolutely vital to their well-being, the more noise and people they see as they begin to grow the more easily they will accept it. Only one type of handling must be banned and that is small children mauling the puppies and picking them up only to drop them when they wriggle. From ten days onwards, weekly puppy nail trimming with a pair of scissors is a kindness to the bitch otherwise they will scratch her as they feed.

Weaning

The pups are very little trouble until weaning begins which can start when they are three weeks old, depending on the supply of the dam's milk and her general condition. Begin with some sort of milky food such as Lactol or one

Eight puppies and eight teats – everyone is happy (Robert Freeman)

of the proprietary brands of puppy milk, mix it as directed, pour it into a flat dish with the pups around it, and smear a little on their noses. In a matter of seconds it will vanish. On the first day feed them once, then increase the number of meals and the quantity gradually. Once you start weaning make the bitch stay away from them for periods during the day and feed them before you let her back to them so that they are not hungry. Once they are fully weaned do not let them grab hold of her for a quick snifter. This will make it impossible for her to get her figure back and droopy tits are inclined to get caught on wire and brambles later on.

After ten days of milky food the pups can start on solids, either one of the puppy foods or minced raw beef given in little balls individually. When they become accustomed to this, watch that your fingers are not included in the meal! Increase quantities gradually, too much too soon will cause scouring. An approximate measure is an ounce of food per pound of puppy weight daily from five weeks onwards, including the milk food. At six weeks it applies to solids only. All-in-one branded puppy foods include all that is necessary and do not need supplementing but if you are old fashioned like me and think that dogs must have good raw meat, then Weetabix, porridge, biscuit meal or brown bread should be soaked and added to the meat together with a vitamin/mineral additive such as Canoval. Fresh water must always be available but not in a dish deep enough for them to get soaked if they stumble into it.

Dosing for roundworms can start from four weeks, using either Antipar, a delicious orange-flavoured syrup, or a powder or tablets. This should be repeated three times at ten-day intervals and again when they are twelve weeks old. As weaning progresses the bitch will be with them less and less until she is only with them at night. She may want to play with them during the day but don't put her with them directly after she has been fed as she is likely to regurgitate her dinner and the pups will gobble it up. Although completely natural, this upsets any control of quantity you may have planned for their diet. Also what the bitch eats is not necessarily suitable for her pups.

Providing the parents are Kennel Club registered a registration form must be acquired from the Kennel Club in order to register the puppies. You can either name each puppy individually or register the litter en masse leaving it to their new owners to name them. This should be done soon after the pups are born so you will have the forms to give to the new owners.

Selling

Time was when much gundog breeding was quite unconnected with commercialism. The object was either to improve the breed, in which case only the best were kept to be bred from, or for the personal benefit of the breeder who culled what he did not need. Perhaps some were given to selected friends but none were put on the open market. I doubt if this happens anywhere today. Puppies are sold if only to cover the cost of breeding a litter in order to supply a replacement for the breeder. Other litters are bred purely for sale. The selling of puppies involves a great responsibility on the part of the breeder, not only in selecting suitable owners but also caring what happens to the dogs in later years. This is not so with many breeders particularly with those who breed commercially. Their responsibility ends the day that the puppy leaves home. Should a mistake be made in assessing the new owner, or a genuine reason why the new owner cannot keep the animal, then interest and help should be given by the breeder to rehouse the little creature which was brought into the world at his instigation. If new owners are desperate to get rid of the dog then some of them are not going to worry too much where the puppy goes. This can result in him being mistreated and unwanted – no caring breeder would want this on his conscience. Every puppy should go to the right home from the beginning if possible.

It is illegal to sell a puppy under six weeks of age, but after that, providing they are fully weaned and the new owner is capable of looking after a tiny puppy, then from seven weeks onwards they can leave home. The older they are the longer they will take to settle into new surroundings away from their brothers and sisters. Imprinting starts very early and the trauma of new faces, voices and surroundings is far greater to a twelve-week-old than to a eight-week-old pup.

On the day of collection have a copy of the pedigree ready together with a KC registration form or transfer of ownership form, a detailed diet sheet plus a small quantity of the particular food that the pup has been weaned onto so that should the new owner want to alter the diet this can be done gradually. Supply a piece of bedding from the nest which will make the first night away from home a lot easier. An unhappy and lonely puppy can always be given half a Disprin to help him go to sleep.

Finally may I say that a reference to the various breed rescue societies gives you an idea of the number of puppies which are bred, sold and then discarded. Don't let this happen to your puppies, breed with care and fore-thought so that you bring into the world a healthy, well-reared litter which will be capable of working either as retrievers, spaniels, pointers or one of the hunt, point, retrieve group. Make sure that you sell them only to people who really want them and will care for them during their working lives, and when this is over will give them a happy and peaceful retirement and finally a quick and painless death when the time comes.

The Bird Dog in the Field

KEITH ERLANDSON

Keith Erlandson started work, after leaving Kingston High School, Hull, as a gamekeeper in 1948 where he learned the old, traditional methods of gamekeeping from Bill Spinks, former head keeper to the Earl of Dudley. In those days pheasants were reared by the labour-intensive system of the open-rearing field and wild pheasants played a very significant part in producing birds to put over the guns. In this era nobody ever had any problems inducing pheasants to fly.

During the next eleven years he developed an interest in gundogs, particularly spaniels, although his first dogs were golden retrievers and labradors. He won his first open spaniel trial on 1 January 1957 and sometime afterwards decided to become a professional gundog trainer, moving to North Wales in 1958 where he has lived ever since. He has competed regularly in spaniel trials and has made up 20 field-trial champions: 15 springers and 5 cockers. He won the spaniel championship for springers in 1960 and 1986 and the cocker championship three years in succession, with the same bitch, FTCh Speckle of Ardoon, in the early seventies, a feat no other spaniel handler or spaniel has ever equalled.

In 1976, his interest extended to pointers and setters and although he has won several field-trial awards with these dogs, he has never become hooked on trials and prefers to shoot over the dogs instead. The fascination is that bird dogs take him to strange, remote and wild places, in pursuit of a truly wild quarry which man cannot reproduce.

Background

The pointer in Great Britain, and also the native setter, has evolved over the past two hundred years plus, and should not be confused with the more recently imported German pointers, which fulfil a function midway between the spaniel and the native pointer. The main ancestor of the pointer, from which comes his air-scenting powers and interest in locating gamebirds, is the old Spanish pointer. The breed was brought to this country in the eighteenth century after the Treaty of Utrecht by serving officers who had fought in the war of the Spanish succession. In his native land the Spanish pointer was a partridge dog, pure and simple. Spanish redlegs down the ages must have behaved far more co-operatively than they seem to do in this country, where they almost invariably run like blazes and hardly ever lie for a pointing dog. In Spain, the redlegs, after being pointed by the Spanish pointers, either were taken with a net drawn over them (although this method was more favoured in France where crouching setters had the net drawn over dog and birds) or shot on the ground with a crossbow, or later in history with an arquebus firing a lead bullet. Shooting flying birds was not a common practice.

The Spanish pointer was a heavy, ponderous animal, not designed for galloping over huge tracts of country but his air-scenting powers were deadly, although his disposition was said to be surly. The British officers, who imported the breed, although appreciating his game-finding ability, required a more mobile, adaptable dog and the credit goes to a Colonel Thornton for 'improving' the Spanish pointer by crossing it with the foxhound. This was *not* done to improve the breed's scenting powers as one present-day writer recently suggested. The Spanish pointer's nose for air scent was second to none, whereas the foxhound is a line hunter. This was actually a disadvantage in these early out-crossings. A pointer must work with a high head at all times, to catch wind-borne bird scent. To drop his nose on foot scent is a fault and counter-productive as a dog with his nose on the ground is incapable of picking up the essential air scent.

The foxhound was introduced to give greater pace, mobility and stamina

Pointer

A springer makes allowance for a steep bank and creeps through

(Overleaf) *A well matched pair of labradors*

Controlling a dog in the beating line in thick cover is never easy

and to produce an altogether more graceful animal and selective breeding played a large part in breeding away from the low-headed traits of the foxhound and maintaining the high-headed characteristics of the original import. Thornton, although recognised as the father of the native pointer, did not do his work unaided. The eighteenth- and nineteenth-century gun-smiths played a large part in the development and improvement of the breed. G.W. Lang of Essex, a descendant of Joseph Lang the gunmaker, informs me that the earlier Lang was responsible for introducing the lemon-and-white colouration, by out-crossing with a Billy, a lemon-and-white hound which originated from Château Billy in France and was used for boar and staghunting.

It is not certain for what purpose the returning British officers brought the Spanish pointer home with them, whether it was for falconry, partridge netting or shooting, or all three, but shooting flying birds certainly became fashionable shortly after the importation of the Spanish pointer. In fact I would venture to suggest that the availability of these dogs did more to popularise wing shooting than any other factor. One of the more famous and colourful characters of the latter half of the eighteenth century, who kept a kennel of pointers, was George, the Prince Regent, and he had a particularly splendid bitch called Juno. She is portrayed by an artist of the day on an intense point, by a broken-down rail fence.

Whenever we read of the shooting exploits of eighteenth and early nine-teenth century sportsmen, such as Squire Osbaldeston, Col Peter Hawker, Coke of Norfolk, Charles St John, Sir Fowell Buxton (the slave-trade aboli-tionist and the restorer to this country of the capercaillie) and Capt Horatio Ross, we can guarantee that their bags of partridges and grouse were made over pointers and possibly setters. Driving game had not come into being, as the breech loader had not been invented and the slow rate of fire of the flintlocks and percussion muzzle-loaders of the period fitted in perfectly with the pointing dogs' method of working. Walking-up in line as we know it was not practised as this is simply a modern way of getting more guns onto the ground for a day's shooting, either to help to pay the shooting rental or to attract more revenue in a commercial enterprise. These early sportsmen did not go in for large shooting parties. Usually they shot alone (apart from the inevitable retainers) or with another gun, as only two guns at the most can cover the dog on point. Dogs were expected to do the groundwork and find the birds for them and it was considered *infra dig* for the sportsmen to tramp birds up out of turnips themselves. They simply shot to enjoy themselves and commercialism was unknown.

Consider the scenario. The gun(s) would set out either on foot or mounted on steady shooting ponies. One gun would be carried by the shooter. A second gun would most probably be carried by a gamekeeper. Another gamekeeper would handle the pointing dogs, running them either singly or in a brace,

Gordon setter on point

according to the whim of the master. The dog would find game and come on rigid point and if two dogs were being used, his bracemate would 'back' on sight, assuming a pointing stance so as not to run into the pointing dog's birds from the flank and flush them prematurely. The guns would walk to the point and position themselves on either side of the dog-handler, who would then quietly order the dog to advance. The dog would draw in slowly, head still well up, never sniffing along the track of moving birds. The covey would explode and the gentlemen would discharge the fowling pieces. They would be given their second guns and the dog, which had dropped to shot, would be ordered to move in again in case any laggards were still lurking. Another keeper with a retrieving dog would collect the fallen birds. The dogs would then be recast onto fresh ground to seek more game. There were variations on this theme. Often a gentleman would shoot alone, handling his own dogs and recharging his own piece, with a single retainer to retrieve and carry the game.

It was the partridge, rather than the grouse, which was the more usual quarry of the pointer during the early years of the breed's development. The reasons are not hard to find. Every English landowner lived on his own estate and although partridges would be more plentiful in the lower rainfall, east-ern agricultural areas, the birds were sufficiently well distributed to provide sport in virtually every part of England. The squire could, therefore, shoot partridges on his own estate without having to travel anywhere else. With the advent of the railways, grouse shooting became more popular simply because those sportsmen who lived in the south were able to make the journey to northern England and Scotland with no difficulty. The resident Scottish lairds had been able to indulge themselves in this sport ever since it became fashionable and the Gordon setter was developed exclusively for this pursuit.

Before the development of the breech-loader, and the new demand for more and more birds to accommodate the new sport of shooting driven grouse, more old growth of heather was tolerated than is now considered to be consistent with optimum grouse production. Tracts of old heather provided useful cover to hold the birds for the dogs and the familiar chequer-board pattern of small burned strips all over the ground which we associate with a good driving moor was unknown in the dogging days. But this was soon to change.

Big bags of driven grouse, partridges and pheasants became fashionable and a hitherto unknown rivalry between the various shoot-owners manifested itself. The pointer will never make record bags no matter how well stocked the ground is, so his employment went into a gradual decline. There are, however, dogging moors in part of Invernesshire, Ross-shire, Wester Ross, Sutherland and Caithness where no matter how intensively the ground is keepered and burned, they will never produce the numbers of birds required for a good day's grouse driving so these areas became the last bastions of the pointers and setters and remain so until this day.

In the south, the transition from shooting partridges over dogs to driven partridge shooting became even more complete and the pointer virtually died out on the partridge manors, and where it existed at all, it was only employed as a grouse dog. Following the mechanisation of the farms came the demand for super-efficient agriculture, with its destruction of hedgerows, weedkillers and toxic insecticides. This new era saw the virtual genocide of the grey partridge, so the bird as a dogging or a driving proposition was negligible; at the present time therefore fewer partridges are shot over pointers and setters than any kind of game shot by any other method.

As happened quite recently in the case of the working cocker spaniel, it was the field-trial people who kept the pointers and setters alive. The field-trial lobby is a strange body. It is a cross-section of humanity and by this token consists of persons with a wide range of differing personalities. I have stayed on the perimeter of field trials for over thirty years, making frequent excursions inwards and carrying off a fair amount of booty over this period, but I have never become fully integrated. However, I believe field trials, though imperfect, have done a great deal of good for gundogs.

At the end of World War II there were few pointers and setters in England but field-trial interest revived. William Humphreys had kept his Dashing Bondhu kennel of Llewelyn setters going over the war years. Lord Rank formed a kennel of pointers at Sutton Scotney and at one period had no fewer than three private professional handlers, Bill Brunt, Davie Monro and Alf Manners. Captain Parlour had a kennel of English setters of mainly Llewelyn bloodlines handled by Tommy Spark. The Lady Auckland of Cromlix had both Gordon setters and pointers, the latter being very successfully handled by Angus McCloughlin. Mrs Florence Nagle and Miss Clark shared a kennel of Irish setters which were handled by the Shropshire maestro George Abbot. George Burgess, the Irishman living in North Wales, carried on with his Gordon setters through thick and thin. Alun Roberts, from Caernarfon, ran his Segontium pointers and a strong Irish contingent always swelled the numbers. Foremost among the Irishmen was John Nash, arguably the leading breeder of, and authority on, the Irish setter worldwide, and no mean hand with a pointer either.

These people bred and ran their dogs in trials when interest in these animals as shooting dogs was at a low ebb. True, Lord Rank shot partridges over his dogs in Hampshire and I believe grouse in Scotland also. Capt Parlour shot grouse over his dogs in Durham and the Irishmen have always had an interest in their trial dogs for everyday shooting purposes

The writer shooting grouse over an English setter

Stanley Smith's pointer FTCh Max Sparkfield of Dorvalston on grouse, backed by Julie Organ's Fernglen Forester

but outside field-trial circles, few of these dogs were kept purely as shooting dogs except for a few places in the far north of Scotland. But the interest of the field-triallers kept the dogs alive and without this interest they would have died out.

Then came a revival in interest in shooting grouse over dogs. The shooting on many Scottish estates became commercialised to help make ends meet and in several cases deer ground was shot which had not been utilised as grouse ground before. The result has been an increase in birds on the hitherto sparsely populated deer ground. Shooting breaks up territorial patterns and accounts for a proportion of old birds which allows more young pairs to take territories. Young birds are not so greedy for ground as old birds, so pair density is marginally increased with a subsequent increase in total population and shootable surplus. Many overseas sportsmen like shooting over dogs, particularly the Italians. The Italians have had a bad press over their shooting activities, both in this country and in the good game country of the Canadian prairies and deservedly so in many cases, but some Italians are excellent sportsmen and very knowledgeable dog men. Italy has tremendous field-trial activity and as good a collection of pointers, setters and handlers as can be found anywhere in the world, but they don't have grouse at home apart from blackgame and some ptarmigan in the Alps, so they like to come over and shoot some in England.

Many field-trial handlers help to supply this need by handling their dogs for shooting parties after the summer trial season has finished. Some estates keep their own dogs and a member of the Whitbread family, who owns a stalking and dogging estate in Wester Ross, keeps his own pointers and Irish setters, so these anachronisms of a bygone age still find employment within the same family.

As an 'estate dog', I believe the pointer scores over all the other breeds. Most are relatively uncomplicated. Few are nervous animals. They do well under a kennel regime and are not so desperate for human company as the German pointer, which is far happier helping to drive the car from the passenger seat than travelling in the dog compartment in the back. There are some really excellent setters and I have seen good examples of all three breeds, English, Irish and Gordon, but as a general rule, they are harder to train.

The best two English setters I have ever seen were FTCh Sharnberry Glenharoo, who was half French with some strong Irish setter characteristics and FTCh Bringwood Caprice but as I write these words, the English setter is at a low ebb in Great Britain, although strong in Scandinavia and Italy. The Irish setter has an elusive and mystical quality which cannot be defined by the written word. Gordon setters have done well in field trials over the past few years and are wide running, efficient game-finders but my shooting experience over this breed is confined to only one animal. The pointer quarters his ground with little on his mind because he is an amiable simpleton and finds his game because he is programmed to do so, whereas the setter quarters his ground, hoping he can find a ridge to disappear over in the anticipation of finding some evil to do when out of sight. By tradition, none of these breeds is used for retrieving in this country in a purist situation. It used to be believed that to allow them to retrieve would make them unsteady to shot or even unsteady on the point itself. This is a view which few have thought fit to challenge. The evidence from some countries abroad, where these dogs are required to retrieve both in field trials and in a shooting situation, negates these theories. In the USA, game is not shot in the National Quail Championship, but in most other stakes the dogs retrieve and every American 'hunter' expects his pointer and setter to retrieve and if they don't retrieve tenderly there won't be much of a quail left to barbeque. In Italy, Sweden and Norway, the field-trial dogs must retrieve and in Italy must complete a water retrieve also. Although these dogs are not specifically bred for their retrieving ability, the truth is that many will retrieve, given the opportunity, and do it well. Irish and Gordon setters have a particularly strong retrieving instinct and I have had more pointers which have been natural retrievers than have not. I seldom allow my bird dogs to retrieve because where I shoot, the going is extremely hard. Most of it is high blanket bog, which is springy and tussocky with severe gradients. When birds are down, I prefer my dogs to conserve their energy rather than expend themselves on looking for shot birds. Also, I usually have a young spaniel I want to educate on retrieving, so I prefer to use the shot birds for this purpose but I do find that if I have a young bird dog which is a bit backward, his interest will be stimulated by letting him find and retrieve a bird or two. In any event, I always let a young dog have a lick of blood from a bird, although I don't care to disfigure my game by pulling the heads off the birds and feeding them to the dog as his reward, as seems to be traditional among American quail hunters.

Hunting Technique

Not one single breeder of pointers and setters deliberately breeds for good mouths in their dogs; however, many do have good mouths if allowed to handle shot game. Irish setters are particularly famed as retrievers, and in Northern Ireland a minority are not used as setters at all but as duck-shooting dogs. In pointers, the Fearn kennel in Ross-shire, owned by Mrs Eppie Buist and Jim Howden, regularly produce excellent retrievers, in fact I believe it would be hard to find a Fearn pointer which is not a natural retriever. Jim Howden has a most amusing cartoon picture of one of their bitches retrieving a grouse and wearing a very smug expression, carrying the bird past an outraged looking bevy of June Atkinson's 'Holway' golden retrievers, whose eyes have just been wiped by the pointer. Nevertheless, I believe retrieving in a bird dog should be looked upon as a secondary function, if at all. Many handlers do not expect their dogs to retrieve but take them close to the fall of the birds and allow them to point the shot birds, which are then picked by hand but even when accurately pointed, a live, tucked-in bird can take some finding in a rough patch of heather. It must never be forgotten that the *raison d'être* of the pointer and setter is to find game and to stay with it until the gun(s) can walk to the dog.

In America, after the dog has pointed and held steady on the birds, his job ends there unless he is required to retrieve after the shot. But the dog is never asked to 'produce' the birds. The handler of the dog, who may or may not be the gun, advances ahead of the dog on point and belabours the cover with a 'flushing whip' in an endeavour to put the birds up. Some Americans claim it is because quail sit very tight early in the season and they don't want the dog to reach in and catch a bird, but our young grouse can sit very tight in July, when several field trials are held and although the odd accident can happen and the occasional grouse is caught, basically dogs cope very well and put up their birds with decorum. I will accept that quail may well lend themselves to the flushing-whip technique but the Americans use their bird dogs on pheasants to a far greater extent than we do on this side of the water (except in Ireland) and a pointed pheasant can run into the next county whilst you are flailing around. For all I know, their sharptail grouse, blue grouse and prairie chickens could be equally mobile, so I would have thought that a dog which would advance steadily along the track of moving birds, never losing contact, could be a valuable asset. This is what is required according to our shooting and field-trial standards but before we consider this final part of the pointer's work, we must consider the moment when the dog is cast off.

Although dogs are sometimes worked downwind and on side winds, the most classic performance is regarded as the beat into the wind. Here the dog is able to work a symmetrical pattern, going flat across the wind, making a U turn at the end of his beat, taking a new chunk of ground which is consistent with prevailing scenting conditions, which a competent dog has already assessed, and crossing the front of the handler again to make a compensatory cast on the other side. When the dog winds game his behaviour may vary according to the variables of the situation. If a covey, barren pair or old single cock has been at rest for some time and a good breeze is blowing, the dog is likely to take the birds well out. He may check his gallop and draw forward, head high, at a steady walk. Don't panic. If he knows his stuff, he

Colin Organ's Irish Setter FTCh Westmolland Wags Wonder

won't draw in too far and flush the birds before the guns can draw level with him. His nose tells him exactly what mood birds are in and how close it is safe to approach before making a solid point. He may then remain on point or he might break his point and draw on again. If birds have started to run and he is advancing to pin them, I don't like to see a handler blow his dog down with the stop whistle in a situation like this. The dog is the fellow with the nose. The handler is renowned for his very poor nose, so he should leave things for the specialist to work out.

Once the dog is really 'on' (and remember he may have been 'on' from the very first whiff) he is commanded to advance to produce the birds. He should advance at a steady walk until birds get up. But he might 'stick' on point; this is a most annoying fault, the dog refuses to move in and engage his birds. The handler will get up to all kinds of antics to try and break the spell. He will make encouraging noises, hop from one side of the dog to the other, stamp the ground and kick the heather. This pantomime is likely to cause birds to run forward and keep on running, eventually becoming fed up and flushing at extreme range. Or the guns can move ahead of the dog and attempt to walk-up the birds. This is considered *infra dig* and whereas you can usually engage a covey this way, the chances of putting up an old single cock are fairly remote, so it follows that a free-roaming dog scores every time over the sticky performer.

Another variation in which the dog establishes his point can be encountered when the dog comes across a bird, or two or three birds, which have only recently dropped in after being previously encountered at another point. Scent will not have had time to generate fully and the scent spread will be strictly localised. The dog will not take the bird(s) nearly so far out as he would in the case of well-rested birds, so, encountering bird scent suddenly, the dog will snap into a rigid point in a split second and very likely with a much lower head elevation than would be the case with birds well out and well rested.

Then there is the all-important question of hunting range. Here it's very much horses for courses. Obviously, the thinner the game is distributed on the terrain, the more ground the dog will need to cover for maximum effectiveness. In a field trial on well-stocked driving moors in Yorkshire or Durham, 70–100yd either side of the handler is sufficient to find birds consistently but under real dogging conditions in the North of Scotland, Wales or Norway a dog would need to cover far more ground. By the same token, when Thomas Coke shot his partridges at Holkham, working the small, well-stocked North Norfolk stubble and turnip fields of the day, a closer working dog which would cover the small fields meticulously from hedge to hedge, but never 'breaking fence' into the next field, would be the horse for the course and the dog of the day.

Satch

JOHN HUMPHREYS

And so to the present, the latest in a line of gundogs which has run unbroken for almost forty years. Kenzie grows old, his muzzle grey, face scarred by who knows how many confrontations with thorn bushes, limbs crooked and twisted after a thousand cold swims and heaving himself up the fenland dyke banks. His successor I came by in rather an unusual way, something of an 'impulse buy'.

I was invited to address the famous Frodsham and District Wildfowling Club's fiftieth birthday dinner, a great honour for me and also a pleasure to travel up to the Dee to visit many old friends. I came back from that occasion with rather more than the rosy glow and the hangover which might have been the conventional after-effects. When I awoke next morning at home it slowly dawned on me that I had also bought a labrador puppy, unseen, from David Griffith, the club president. Like chainsawing, tightrope walking and scything, dog-buying is a serious business and ought to be conducted only by the stone-cold sober. However, the deed was done and we spent the following day dog-proofing the garden and upmarketing the run and kennel accommodation. Kenzie had come to know and respect his boundaries but a lively puppy would be through the gaps and under the fence in no time. With a pair of pliers, bandaged fingers and two sons on hand to offer advice and criticism the deed was done. I would defy a quite small and infirm tiger to escape from the garden now.

We bought a new feeding bowl, a course of worm pills, brand new slip lead, new kennel and all that was necessary. Claire Griffith and I met at a suitable midway point between North Wales and Cambridgeshire, the summit conference took place and the transfer fee changed hands. The die was cast.

I need not have worried. Rechristened Satch, a name which any jazz buff will appreciate but also one short enough to be roared effectively in thick cover, the newcomer was a little dear. I was about to enter a new era of gundog ownership for which the previous run of ruffians, Rambos, macho hounds and psychopaths which have lived at my expense for the last thirty years had ill prepared me.

Life with Kenzie had made me forget many things which were possible. Satch walked to heel! He sat! He looked to me for advice and encouragement and exhibited unusual traits of good manners, courtesy and a desire to please. This was an experience to savour. What is more, this paragon was already immune to sheep, chickens, cows, other dogs and mopeds, so clearly renaissance was at hand.

Some anxieties remained. How would Kenzie react to the interloper, a bouncy, disrespectful newcomer to share his garden, kennel, run, shady spot near the shrubbery, bones and other personal treasures over which he held proprietorial rights? He has his crotchety moments, no more than to be expected of a semi-retired military man who, when faced by an intrusion into everything in life he considered sacred, might cut up rough. However, Kenzie is not sensitive enough to take offence and his ugly, good-natured face beamed a panting welcome through the bars of the gate so that hurdle was over: Satch was installed. It took a day or two for Kenzie to grasp the idea that Satch was not a toy boy provided by me for his sexual gratification and that any such relationship was doomed, and after a few misunderstandings they settled down to peaceful, platonic co-habitation.

I was luckier than I deserved, for Satch could pluck a biscuit from between Kenzie's lips and, far from taking offence, Kenzie regarded the liberty as no more than a puckish jest and peered round myopically on the grass to see where the morsel had gone. Before I could intervene, Satch would thrust his head into Kenzie's very feeding bowl but again, there was not so much as a growl from the old monster nor a pause in the frenzied wagging of that scythe-blade of a tail.

Oddly enough, as the training advanced, Kenzie seemed to become better behaved. He too started sitting, walking to heel impeccably and conducting himself as though his previous decade of misconduct was but a figment of the imagination. All too late to do any good, of course, but it was an interesting second childhood, for all that. If only he had behaved thus six years ago. Although I had prepared separate sleeping accommodation they preferred to muck in together, snuggling down like two intertwined ebony carvings, a Rodin sculpture in black marble.

A new dog is a fresh start, a chance to make good all the mistakes you made last time and to anticipate problems instead of merely reacting to them after they have appeared. The memories, the joys and sorrows of puppy ownership return all too quickly. Lost slippers, torn washing, rape of my garden pondweed, unexpected excavations in the flower beds, stumbling over a soft and yielding figure in the dark and the 'look-at-me-aren't-I-clever' look as he drags his bedding round the lawn.

Again, full of new optimism, I embark on a new adventure with a fresh dog; no doubt he will prove different from all his predecessors in this way or that and will develop strengths and weaknesses which none of them possessed. Time will tell. After him, no doubt will come another dog, then another until my shooting days are over. I hope it will not be for a long time as gundog work, for all its heartbreak, worry and hard work is one of the real delights of shooting, and for all my tribulations, I would not have been without any one of those which have shared my life since that far-off day when old Simon retrieved my first flying pigeon.

The Advanced Gundog

DIANA DURMAN-WALTERS

Diana Durman-Walters is a professional dog trainer who began her career as a primary school teacher. Ten years ago she decided to run a full-time training kennel for gundogs and today they occupy her time totally. In addition she is co-director of the Scottish Academy of Falconry and Related Studies situated in the Border country.

Falconry and shooting require gundogs of talent and ability and Diana has trained a large variety of breeds for clients requiring them for one or other of these disciplines as well as training for field trials. At present she has one of the best known kennels of imported German wirehaired pointers used in the field, and stock from Diana has entered into some of the most prestigious homes in Great Britain. She is very fortunate that the surrounding countryside is ideal for advanced dog training and this environment has produced some outstanding dogs under Diana's tutelage.

Today she is busier than ever with the upsurge of interest in gundogs, particularly with the increase in continental gundog work. This has meant a greater variety of dogs to work with and, as she herself admits, you never stop learning in this profession.

To the casual onlooker or aficionado, the skills of the advanced trained gundog leave you full of admiration. Stopping at the faintest hint of a whistle command, turning on cue and returning on recall with all afterburners going, it sits and waits avidly for the next command, having just delivered the most spectacular retrieve. How do we get a dog like that? I hear distraught captains of shoots or head keepers cry. So what's the problem? One of the main reasons that we don't all possess a dog of this calibre is that not enough attention was

Dogs in the shooting field should not be competitive

given to detail in the early stages of advanced training. It's very easy to slip into the old adage, 'Well at least the dog is enjoying himself' as he creates unstoppable havoc in the release woods, or puts up game miles in front of the nearest gun, who by now has got the second barrel on a canine target with the thought of at least getting something in the bag!

All dogs that have been through a basic training programme are capable of completing advanced skills. To what degree they achieve this depends on their receptiveness and the thoroughness of the training itself. The breed of the dog doesn't matter as they all have to perform the same rituals in the field and all respond to discipline and trainer efficiency.

At the present moment shooting is enjoying a tremendous upsurge with people from home and abroad wishing to spend their leisure time in this pursuit. One of the changes that springs immediately to mind is the demand for walked-up grouse shooting. This can be done either with labrador or springer, or more excitingly over 'bird dogs' (pointers, setters) and HPRs. It is now more common to see guns who are spending time on upland gamebirds in the autumn coming down to the lowland gamebirds in early winter. These migratory sportsmen often need dogs to perform on many types of terrain and will need to train their dogs for a wider variety of skills.

Upland Gamebirds

Grouse

Red grouse and black grouse represent the two most common gamebirds sought by northern sportsmen. Ptarmigan are often too high for most guns to want to climb for, and very often are too tame to warrant attention. By far and away red grouse make the most demands on the dogs and guns alike. Spread over vast tracts of ground that will need to be walked over for many hours, it becomes a test of fitness all round. For those of us who choose to run our own dogs it is more than likely that we will have a pointer/retriever for the job as we can utilise this breed once we start on the low ground. They do not have the speed of the pointers and setters but as medium-paced dogs they can cover the ground and have great powers of endurance, being more heavily built. The general idea is that we want the dog to quest and search for singletons or coveys of grouse, stop and point, flush and retrieve, preferably in that order! In the meantime we are giving our concentration 100 per cent to the departing grouse, giving them our best shots and not worrying whether the dog is giving a very good imitation of a coursing event. He, of course, is awaiting the next command. And so he should be.

Before any novice dog is introduced to grouse work, particularly if he is an HPR, it is far better that the initial work has been done on partridge and/or pheasants. The scent of these birds is much more delicate and resistant to detection. A dog will need to work harder at location because contour distractions such as hedges, bushes, trees and even tussocks of grass deflect the scent, requiring greater powers of concentration from the dog. In addition he'll need to make decisions as to whether the game is running in front, or is this the trail of a bird behind, or one that has departed? One of the major problems with running pointers and HPRs on the low ground is rabbits. If the ground has a fair smattering of these, then the dog will be inclined to want to keep his head low to the ground to locate them. Too much of this work will produce a low head carriage and will teach him to be a 'foot scenter'. Instead of keeping his head held high for air scents he deems it necessary to run with his head cutting the daisies, so to speak. In the bleak world of heather-covered hills and crags the only favourable scent he is likely to locate quickly will be above the canopy of the heather.

Here the drifting scents of grouse are then explored and precisely located. With the higher head carriage comes a greater ability to explore bigger tracts of ground, hence lessening expending energy unnecessarily. When you look at a dog endlessly quartering a moor you begin to realise that he is weaving a very thin, thread-like path as he quests for grouse. The clockwork patterns of low-ground work become a little superfluous here. The dog by throwing his head into the wind has the ability to detect scent that has been diluted by thousandths of a degree. It's wonderful to watch a dog that has located a fragment of scent throw his head up higher and swing into the stream of the scent without breaking pace, then suddenly lock on point.

Naturally when all is said and done you don't want your dog to have locked on point three-quarters of a mile away, meaning that you'll need fresh supplies of oxygen to reach him. As you begin to walk the moor you must have a predetermined beat or area that you would like him to work in. Mentally make a picture of 100yd either side of you so that he does not run beyond this. It's nothing short of daunting to have to walk continuously over the moor to a dog miles away. Keep him within range. If you're not sure what 100yd looks like then take a look at your local school running track. Take a good look at the 100yd finishing line. Now you've got your mark.

Of course he will not want to stay within those limits and so you'll have to enforce this. Using the whistle command allow him to run out to within the 100yd barrier and turn him into the opposite direction. The command I use is two pips and a hand signal for the direction. There's a good chance he'll listen to start with then start 'pulling-on', that is, attempting to work beyond the agreed limit. Once he does this *stop him*. Using the stop whistle command blow him down. Wait until he's watching you then with your arm out clearly in the direction he must take, give him the turn whistle and cast him across. It is at moments such as these that you remain patient, as he is more than likely to have a notion in his head to defy you and continue the way he was going when you blew him down. It is very important that he turns to see what you want him to do, as if he doesn't then there is a very strong chance that he'll simply take off into the distance as soon as you give him a command. If he makes a move to continue the way *he* wanted to go immediately stop him once more. Now, of course, you'll need to have done your basic training correctly. Can you command this dog at a distance when there is a clash of wills? Is he going to listen to you, after all you can't reach him from there can you? If it appears that you are not going to be able to give a command at a distance simply because he is trying it on then go up to where he is sitting, pick him up and shake him vigorously. In others words smarten his ideas up. This is usually just what the doctor ordered and even you will be surprised at the about turn he'll make and co-operate with you. Don't ever be afraid to correct your dog when in company. Most people I know much prefer to have a good day's sport provided by a suitably chastened dog than to have it ruined by a dishonest dog running amok.

When you are running a young dog, sometimes it is profitable to allow an older dog to do the retrieving. This allows the novice to spend as much time as possible perfecting his hunting and pointing. All too quickly they learn the art of 'running-in' and picking up game to retrieve. This of course is very dangerous when you are shooting over dogs. All too quickly they can become the target, as they enter into the pattern of shot. During the first season novices must emphatically be told to 'sit' and 'stay'. If the dog has been taught to drop to shot then without question he should hit the ground like a stone and stay there in the lying down position. If on the other hand you feel confident in sending him for the retrieve then stand where you are and direct him to the fall. Don't be tempted to go to the spot yourself looking for the bird (with the dog doing frantic circles round you looking for the same thing). Once you have entered the 'fall' area you are effectively about to wipe out the scent for him. With your feet eroding scent like a herd of elephants going through the bush you'll mask all available scent and probably end up with no bird at all. If you have some time to kill then stop for a short while to allow scent to accumulate. This will be of enormous benefit and will help in a difficult retrieve. Heather also manages to cover up the scent of grouse by large deposits of pollen. This fine powdery substance, consisting of numerous fine grains, ends up adhering to the mucous linings of the nose. It can be very noticeable when you look round and see your dog has a green/yellow nose! Undoubtedly this effectively renders the dogs 'supersense' of smell diminished. His pointing may begin to falter and his retrieving may suffer because he cannot fetch what should be a comparatively easy find. Pollen seems to be most actively floating about when it is a particularly warm day with plenty of light wind scudding it about. Warm, sunny days seem the worst. What appears a glorious carpet of burning purple as far as the eye can see will be

A charming team of golden retrievers

a nightmare for the dogs. On days such as these you must ensure that your dog is not the only one to run. Not only will you break his style and pace, as you will tax him beyond endurance, but the accumulation of pollen will force him to make too many mistakes. It makes sense to have at least three good dogs in the team which allows each dog forty minutes rest for twenty minutes 'burn-out' every hour.

Sometimes the ground that you have to walk over in search of grouse is only marginal. Here it is quite possible to hunt springer spaniels letting them quest back and forth helping you to put up the game. Forestry ground often requires these tenacious little workers to hunt out tussocky areas between the timber line and the heather patches. Because the ground is more likely to have white grass areas on it the tighter range of the spaniel allows a more consistent pattern of work in smaller heather zones. In particular if you have to work in and out of the trees you would find the spaniel much more of an asset than a pointer as you wouldn't worry as to whether he was on point somewhere in there. If you've chosen to take your labrador to the hill then ensure that he walks to heel letting the hunting breeds do the work. These specialist retrievers work best at their job of picking-up. No breed does it better. Letting him get out to hunt for birds will bring its own problems later on when you are trying to contain him at the 'peg' on one of your pheasant shoots. With all the action going on around him he'll be reluctant to sit there just for picking-up. It's the same old problem of 'horses for courses'.

Because of the tight structure of their feathers, grouse make good retrieves. The youngster doesn't have the problem of feathers coming out (like woodpigeons) and it is just the right size for the smaller spaniels through to the larger pointer/retrievers to gather up and fetch back. Because they are so compact there is a temptation to send a novice retriever for them before enough work has been done on 'cold game'. Young dogs coming upon grouse for the first time are very tempted to seize this mouth-sized item in too firm a hold. This can damage the bird and render it unfit for the table. With all the pressure of the hunt, then the flush, it's not surprising that the dog doesn't want it to get away after all that! Hence the aggressive attitude to retrieving. For a novice still being tutored in retrieves the most sensible thing to do as stated earlier is to let the proven dogs fetch. At the end of the morning, or afternoon put a cool grouse out into the heather and set up a retrieve lesson.

Sit the dog down with the word 'mark'. Throw the grouse into the heather approximately 30yd from the dog, preferably into the wind so that he attempts this with confidence. With your arm outstretched give him the command of 'lost' and cast him on. He should run directly to the spot where it landed and pick it up, particularly since it has your scent on it. Encourage him to make a direct retrieve with the word 'heel' or 'here' and point to the ground. This then does not allow him to play around with the retrieve and instils into him that this is a serious part of the day. Sometimes dogs are

German wirehaired pointer on point – and locked on!

harassed into damaging birds on the retrieve. Their handlers in eagerness to get them to find it continuously tell them 'seek there', 'hie lost', 'lost there', 'fetch' and just about any other form of beseechment that comes to mind until the dog is overcome with the barrage of words and anxiety of not being able to find it, so that when he does he simply dives onto it, grabs it roughly up, for a none too delicate retrieve. Keep calm and speak to the dog only if it's necessary. If he can't complete the retrieve then it's too difficult for him at present. It is wiser to get your friend to bring his dog over to find the bird than make mistakes with yours that will be difficult to correct.

Dogs that have dual roles are comparatively new breeds. The mastery of their training takes longer than most others. During the Victorian era when the Glorious Twelfth meant the great treks from the south to the fabulous lodges of Sutherland and Caithness, kennels were bursting at the seams with large packs of pointers and setters. Shooting over pointers was *de rigueur*. Teams of up to twelve dogs ran the vast moors locating grouse for the guns. Dogs learned to run in brace speeding up the action somewhat. Pointers and setters were capable of retrieving, which they did most successfully, but this aspect of their work was phased out when breeding programmes concentrated on style, speed, and classic pointing. It was found that by using spaniels to flush the grouse you could concentrate on breeding superb running machines whose only function was to find and point birds. The nose of these dogs was everything.

Little has changed in the interim years for the pointers and setters. They are now enjoying a revival with the popularity of walked-up grouse over pointers. The devotion to the various breeds has been very much in the hands of the field triallist. They have maintained the high standard of presentation within the breeds. These dogs are only at their best when out on the hill. Gordon, English and Irish setters or English pointers all run with speed and endurance. Their speed, for which they have no equal, and style of pointing are classical. However attractive these breeds may appear they are not for the novice handler. It is often said that if you have one of these breeds then you should have no other, as it takes time to fathom these dogs out and once you've mastered them stick with them.

It is noticeable that the pointer and English setter normally have a large amount of white on them as background colour. This, more than any other feature, makes it very easy to spot them when they point. As the range of these dogs often exceeds other breeds then it is important to be able to locate the dogs quickly once they stop. The dark self-colours of the Irish and Gordon setter don't make it as difficult to spot them as you might think. Their profile stands out well against the contours of the moor. By comparison the ticked coats of broken colour of the HPRs make them very difficult to locate if you haven't been watching where they are running. They blend into the heather, beautifully camouflaged.

Training

As the retrieving aspect of the pointer/setter is latent in the breed it will come as no surprise that they will often be prepared to do just that when out grouse shooting. As with any singular specialist they will not achieve the high standard of retrieving that labradors and springers will attain. Hence it will be necessary, as it was in the Victorian era, to use a second string to your bow. Because you are teaching your pointer to do only one thing (run and point) the way in which you approach this is important. Quartering ability with purpose is essential. Discipline must be exact as must good ground to run the dog on. As with the early training the low ground presents the best training ground for the pointer. By using fields that contain partridge, preferably those that are bordered by hedges, dry stone walls or fences, begin by casting the dog into the wind. Don't be tempted to walk too fast. Let the dog work. The pattern that you are attempting to create is virtually that of 'tram-lines' from edge to field edge. The exactitude of working a field in this way will mean that the dog should not miss any ground that contains birds. Because the fields are bordered, once the dog has reached the edge you can use the 'turn' whistle and will develop in the dog the feeling of distance, that is how far he is allowed to run. Boundaries to fields are excellent training material as they provide a natural barrier so not only can you turn the dog you can stop him as well.

It is very important to run inexperienced dogs into the wind, as they will almost surely 'bump' birds (put them up) if allowed to run with the wind at their backs. Running downwind comes with experience. Pointers have noses of renown. They tend to stand well back off their quarry and are often termed 'long nosed'. This means that their noses are more acute than dogs which have to get in closer before they are sure they have a bird in front. Because of their long nose you may well find that your sitting partridge is not near the pointing dog at all, but anything up to 20–30yd away! Once the dog has been commanded to flush he must drop immediately the birds are away. This, of course, precludes him running-in and makes him reliable on the hill, when out shooting.

Backing, which means honouring the point of another dog, is something which comes easily to them. What is required is that should a second dog running at the same time point first, the other dog must stop immediately and honour him. This is an absolutely breathtaking sight and will be one of the memories of the moor. These dogs also come very much into their own if taken onto forestry ground for blackcock. Although to a purist it might not be ethical to break the stride of these good quarterers they nevertheless would be the dogs to use where large areas of furrowed, planted ground exist. They can make light work of heavy going. Blackcock that are just inside the treeline can be easily disturbed by people coming towards them, hence with the wide-ranging pointer this would make location and potential shots easier to come by. As with all forms of training it is always far better if you are working the dog yourself, and not involved with the shooting, in particular when guns are relying on your dog to provide birds. He should be able to cover the line of guns from left to right and to enable him to be effective in this category, you should take control of the line not allowing them to march on regardless of what the dog is attempting to do for them.

When the dog comes on point take your nearest two guns quietly over to the dog, one on either side. With yourself at the helm, tell the dog to get in. He may, in fact, begin to creep forward slowly and determinedly but not it might appear with birds in front. With the guns move forward with the dog, which more than likely has his birds, although not where he first located them – he will still be in contact. The grouse may have 'run on'; once they are aware of intruders they're not going to sit still for long. From anywhere from 5 to 30yd in front the grouse may break. This will no doubt catch the guns unaware but it's surprising how quickly they learn to 'read' the dog.

With yourself in close contact with the dog there should be no room for error. He will, of course, be sitting as soon as the first shot rings out, waiting for his next command. If he's a pointer or setter, then spaniels or labradors will do the retrieving. If he's HPR then you may wish to send him for the retrieve. With your grouse in the bag nothing is more rewarding than knowing you've trained your dog to this standard and he's a pleasure to be with.

Lowland Gamebirds

Pheasant and Partridge

Lowland birds are a different ball game. Guns are often working in quite difficult terrain, particularly where rough shooting or wildfowling is the norm. For those of us lucky enough to have driven partridge or pheasant, we will require our dog purely for retrieving purposes. In this capacity the breeds best suited for the job are the orthodox retrievers, followed by the spaniels, and possibly some of the HPR family. As a 'peg' dog you should have elected to train a labrador, golden retriever, or perhaps a flatcoat. These dogs have enormous capacity for remaining stationary and quiet whilst in the thick of the action. Because their task is to 'collect' and hunting *per se* doesn't come into it, their memory banks are being flooded with locations of birds on the ground. Needless to say a dog that is whining, howling, or constantly told to 'sit' or 'stay', cannot be concentrating on the fallen birds. Generally much of the work to be done will be straightforward but is more likely to be testing if you have to walk a root field shooting birds in front.

These dropped birds will prove, in some cases, quite a handful as a retrieving exercise particularly if they are runners. The transition from novice to advanced dog takes an enormous leap here. Nothing but practical experience will enable the dog to locate the bird. In this case it is important to be able to direct the dog to 'go back'. You want him to be able to cover different ground particularly if he cannot find the bird at the fall site. A dog can at times be most stubborn in his efforts to find the bird, refusing to negotiate fresh territory, convinced it must somehow be lying where his eyes last told him. At times such as these he must be told to 'sit', then told to 'go back'. Much of the early dummy training now comes into play as he will eventually begin to see the point of this lesson. You should be able to send him back in the early stages up to 30yd away in an attempt to help him relocate the blood scent. If it's a stone-dead bird he will need to work with drive and determination in the dense cover of roots, locating his bird and making a good swift delivery. There is nothing more aggravating than the dog that stops at every plant and bush to mark it, or drops the retrieve he was sent for, dashing off to collect a bird that has just been shot. When his job is complete, recall him to heel and allow the 'maids of all work' the spaniels to take over.

As pheasants are likely to run down the drills away from people the busy, frenetic work of the springer can cause havoc if they are allowed to trail these birds, as I recall only too well. We had been asked this particular day by the head keeper to keep our dogs back, and for some beaters to mind their language as this day's guns were landed gentry. They (the gentry) had elected to walk a root field as one or two of them had brought dogs which they wanted to work. Beater, gun, beater, gun, we lined at the top of the field. Some of the beaters had surreptitiously put pieces of baler twine around the dog for a lead. No one was more surprised than the dog who'd probably never been on one until that moment! The gent next to me smiled and noticing that my dog was sitting, beckoned his springer to do so. The springer obviously had some misgivings about this command as he stood in front three drills away, tongue out, wagging his tail, looking alert and ready for the off. The owner implored him again to sit but at this point we were off and walking. The springer, sensing the occasion, leapt forward another three drills and having decided he'd given these enough attention, took a line down the nearest drill. This time, uproar from the gent. The dog's name was roared out, first politely, then with venom, at which the spaniel stopped, regarded him in a knowing way and carried on. At this point pheasants began to exit from the field all out of gun range. The spaniel was by now doing a good impression of a gazelle, over the tops of the turnips with the owner's blood pressure rising at every step. A bird was then shot to the right. The springer realising the time was right for retrieving went in hot pursuit. Crossing the field at an exceptional rate of knots, he leapt the dry-stone wall and disappeared after the bird. The owner told the field to halt 'we have a bird down', and face now scarlet (which wasn't due to fresh air) took off after the dog shouting strange words in Anglo Saxon, which could have been the dog's surname, and he too disappeared over the dyke wall. Moments later, we could hear the good gent reading out

the riot act and a suitably chastened dog with owner joined the rest of the field; this time dog on the end of some stout baler twine, sympathetically given in a gesture of solidarity from one of the beaters. It can happen to the best of us.

When dogs are in the line of guns, in a field of crop cover, there is always the tendency for the line to walk too fast. Probably the guns treat this as a day out and are just sauntering along, or they're genuinely not aware of how methodical the dog work has to be in order to produce birds. In truth the best moments are to be had when there are only two or three guns out for a day's rough shooting. In this capacity the dog will be in his element, whether he is HPR or spaniel, these are the dogs that are perfectly adapted. The busy, purposeful quartering of the springer spaniel will leave no stone unturned as head down he investigates the cover. As pheasants have a greater tendency to sit tight in brambles and bushes the dog will be required to work methodically so that he doesn't miss game. The spaniel should be kept in close so that the guns are able to take their shots within range. This may seem rather obvious yet a dog working at a wide range is more likely to be pushing the game further and further away so that eventually a flush is made that isn't to anyone's advantage.

Because pointer/retrievers are able to indicate in a very visual way, by remaining rigid, that they have game in front, they are often allowed too much freedom in a wood or game crop. It's assumed that they will come on point and you can walk over to them for the shot. They too like the spaniels need to be contained in restricted areas so that their work is done systematically. Quartering is a quintessential ingredient that allows every other function to fall into a meaningful tableau. Without it there would be chaos. Keep the dog within 20yd either side of you with the guns to either side and walk forward only when the dog has covered the ground in front of you. He should be kept close in front approximately within 15–20ft to give him a chance to investigate. One thing that he will not necessarily be required to do is crawl into cover. The olefactory senses of HPRs are such that their detection capacity allows them to quest available scent from the outside of cover. Spaniels, by comparison, need to enter cover as their job is to 'spring and flush'. Heavy cover over large areas requires HPRs with coat, and in this capacity the German wirehaired pointer comes into his own. The harsh, dense 'wire' coat protects him from the thorniest brambles and tangles of deep cover and like the spaniels (with their good strong coats) he is not afraid to get into the thick of it. One of the jobs he will be expected to perform is to flush on command if he is on point in the deep cover and you are not able to see him. You'll know he's on point as it will go very quiet all of a sudden. As you will be unlikely to enter the cover yourself, you'll need him to get on and flush. Dogs that have had previous experience in working unsighted will do this, therefore the trainer will need to set this situation up before the dog gets into this problem. The problem is that HPRs become used to being in sight of the handler. Once the handler is not visible and the dog is locked on point he becomes reluctant to make the flush even though he's clearly heard the command. Possibly the game is sitting too tight and won't move or the dog has made an attempt to flush and the game still won't move. He'll be reluctant to do too much more in case he makes mistakes. After all you have taught him not to 'peg' game. Often rattling the bushes will be sufficient to spur him on to flush. Be very careful that it's not a rabbit bolting as, odds on, the dog may well be right behind it. Don't shoot until you can see where the dog is.

A good water dog is essential to the wildfowler

It's often assumed that any dog will do when out shooting woods and cover, that all you require is one to put up the game. After all is said and done terriers will enter cover just as successfully and bolt game. Thus it was that I came to meet Dinsdale Piranha. He of the apt name and debatable lineage. Purchased as a Jack Russell, he kept on growing until he resembled a smooth fox-terrier. His long legs meant that he could outstrip other dogs through the woods, which he seemed hell bent on doing most times. Driven by a strong desire to locate pheasants and rabbits in the fastest time possible, he became the only dog I know that every one knew the name of before the end of the drive! Dinsdale had been the original name but Piranha had been a succinct afterthought. He took no prisoners, often leaving his retrieves lying deep in the wood somewhere, for others to find. He could be heard and later seen giving rabbits a run for their money across the next two fields. However if you wanted to preserve your pheasants then Dinsdale was the dog of choice. He could sweep through a wood driving pheasants back away from the guns and just to let you know his geographical location he would begin his manic yapping, which ebbed and flowed depending on how deep the wood was. It says much for the tolerance of the guns towards this (not so little) terrier whose exploits provided amusing diversions to the day. One thing was certain; he was not the dog for the job.

Wildfowling

One sport in particular that requires silence is wildfowling. Dogs that can remain still and quiet are *sine qua non*. One thing that needs taking into consideration is the colour of the dog. Black, solid liver, or dark-ticked dogs will be the ones of choice. Dogs with white on them tend to give the game away and can often inadvertently turn ducks away from flight ponds. Dogs that feel the cold are most likely to fidget and object to being there. One of the methods that I use for retriever training is to do some dummy work in the twilight or at night so that the dog only locates the dummy by sound. He has to listen for the thud as it hits the ground and be sent to retrieve in the dark. This helps him to make positive audible location when at the flight ponds or by the river. This type of training becomes important if the dog has to be sent immediately a duck is down particularly in the river. Where geese are concerned it may be necessary, at times, to take the dog for retrieves you can't make yourself. Dogs that are not afraid of distance swimming are required, in addition to being strong and powerful enough to lift and hold a goose, and retrieve it. Not an easy task.

Wood pigeon

Decoy shooting at pigeons also requires much the same mental attitude from the dog. It can be very much a waiting game and the dog will be required to locate and retrieve birds that are loose feathered and irritating to the mouth.

Before the dogs are taken out on pigeon days they require plenty of practice on 'cold game' retrieves. I normally take a woodpigeon from the freezer, allow it to defrost completely and put it into a leg of an old pair of tights. Leaving the head poking through and the tail sticking out, tie the tights round the neck and the vent. Set up a retrieving lesson which involves some dummy work but more importantly the wrapped pigeon. As the feathers readily detach from the body, they can turn a good retriever into a dog that will refuse pigeons or will begin to mouth the bird because of the irritation set up by the feathers. Instructing the dog in the early programme shows him how to pick up the birds, hence gaining confidence, slowly progressing to the real thing. Once the dog has shown that he treats the pigeon lesson as he would any other form of retrieving lesson, then he's set to be taken out to the fields. I prefer to allow youngsters, new to pigeon shooting, only to retrieve a couple of birds first time round. Usually, friends with dogs are only too keen to do the majority of the picking-up and this in turn allows your dog not to become wholeheartedly sickened by too many pigeons. The golden rule with training the dog for any discipline is don't overdo it.

Rabbits

If ever there was anything that offered the greatest distraction to a dog it is the rabbit. These sirens of the pasture and woodland beckon on the steadiest of dogs with their invitation to the chase. For dogs that are worked on ground where rabbits are a regular feature, steadiness can be instilled

Irish water spaniel

A duck shooter's dog needs to be impervious to bad weather

on a constant basis. Unfortunately, myxomatosis has denuded many areas where once rabbits were abundant, so it is more likely that rabbits will only be encountered infrequently. For a dog working under these conditions it is better that some work is done before he comes upon his first one lying out sunning, and decides that today is a good time to get in shape for the White City stadium.

HPRs normally give prior warning that they have located something by their point. This gives the advantage to the handler to approach the dog with the word 'steady' and to be right on top of him when the command to flush has been made. Should the dog make any attempt to reverse all the rules of previous training then this can be neatly nipped in the bud by enforcing your demands and rapping out the command of 'no'. A dog in the preliminary stages of training would be unlikely to want to listen to a verbal command but as he is now advancing and co-operating on a much higher level the spoken word is often sufficient to get the message across. With breeds that are more likely to flush without the clear visual signals of the pointer then a chase is often imminent.

It will take time for you to become familiar with the nuances of movement that make reading spaniels so important. One method that I use that can be effective is to go ferreting with friends whilst I take the dog along too. He can be put onto a lead whilst the rabbits are being bolted and the 'no' command enforced repeatedly. Rabbit pens which are often used by professional trainers are not available to the majority but they, of course, simulate discovery of rabbits in cover. When a dog is unsighted and puts a rabbit up then it's odds on that these are the occasions that will tempt the dog the most. If familiarity breeds contempt then that is what we are trying to achieve. Steadiness to rabbits is so very important, not because we don't enjoy watching the dog chase the varmint but that in his efforts he may get shot. As rabbits tend not to sit too far away from the warrens, the tendency is to take the shot as soon as one has bolted; should the dog be right behind it then accidents will happen.

Deer Tracking

One of the most exacting of disciplines is that of deer tracking. This form of work may well come into the sportsman's calendar and interest him in some initial training of the dog in the process. Roe deer provide the greatest need for a tracking dog as dense areas of forest hide the beast so that no man could possibly locate a wounded animal without a dog. With deer tracking the most popular dogs are the HPRs. These versatile hunting breeds have been bred to track blood scents for up to (and in some cases over) 700yd. The old Bavarian and Hanoverian schweisshunds which were developed along similar lines to bloodhounds are renowned trackers, still used in Germany and Austria today. However, their heavy frame and singular speciality made it necessary

A sight to gladden the eye of the beholder

to develop the tracking technique in a more versatile dog. They were super-seded by the ubiquitous German wirehaired pointer. Not that these dogs performed the task better; but they could track to a high degree of proficiency and could also be utilised for a wide variety of shooting requirements.

The work of blood tracking doesn't begin until the dog is 18–24 months old. This work requires high levels of concentration and previous discipline, therefore the advanced gundog will only be expected to achieve these skills when he has proven dexterity in the field. The objects needed will be: dried deer skin, or fresh skin or fresh carcass; dried lung or fresh tripe pieces, for rewards; ½pt deer's blood or bull's blood with 1tsp salt added, stirred well then stored in the freezer; stick with 2in × 2in piece of sponge nailed onto the bottom; bucket; dog's leather collar and 20yd long line or more.

Begin by taking your bucket with some of the blood in it and with your stick and sponge you are going to dab a zigzag trail of approximately 100yd. This trail will be on a green field with the grass short so that everything will be as simple as possible. It is very helpful if you take half a dozen short sticks, already sharpened, to mark the trail as you make it. You cannot be sure if the dog is following exactly once you have left the area and it is important from the start that he works without your interpretation of the trail. Leave a stick at the beginning of the trail and go and get the dog. Bring him into the field and sit him about 6ft away from the start. Put his collar on, then attach the line to it, passing the line under the left foreleg. This allows the dog to work without putting undue pressure on his throat. The preparation of putting on the collar signifies to him that something special is to begin and in time he will realise that no other form of hunting must take place. Leave him sitting and go and kneel down as if to examine the trail yourself. His curiosity will consume him. Now go and get him and bring him to the start. Point to the ground and allow him to sniff the blood scent, encourage him to go slowly forward and paying out the line let him discover the path. On no account must he charge forward as if hunting a 'runner', he must learn to take his time and work slowly and methodically. To help him on his way you could lay small rewards for him. Small pieces of tripe or dried deer lung concealed on the trail under small pieces of grass or leaves make the 'hunt' interesting. At the end of the path leave a good piece of reward for his endeavours.

It won't take a dog long to master this first attempt so then he will need a more difficult track. This time set the trail downwind laid by someone other than yourself. Ensure that the blood spots are only one every 6ft and that a deer skin or carcass is at the end with a big reward on top of it. The zigzag trail must be marked as you will not know where it is and rewards can be left as before. Bring the dog forward with the same ritual of putting on the collar and examining the trail. Should he this time steer off the trail and try wind scenting he will probably be lost very quickly. Stop him, pick him up and put him back at the point where he became confused. Cast him on and let him continue. As he gets each reward on the trail praise him well. Finally when it is complete and he reaches the deer make a big fuss of him. Once he is competent at this, set your trails in woodland, begin to encourage him to locate the deer, the last 20–30ft without you on the line, and encourage him to take you back to the deerskin. As he accomplishes this extend the distance.

It is not profitable to attempt this type of work more than once or twice per week in the initial stages. If the dog begins to get bored with this work he will be of little use to you in location operations as he will baulk at the task before him. Hot, dry weather is another no-go area. If he is finding it difficult to keep cool and scenting conditions are poor he will not complete the track. It is known that a dog tracking over 700yd will inhale and exhale over eleven thousand times. The effort involved is arduous and concentration is at a maximum. To work to this high degree of skill demands your patience in training and attention to detail. When the time comes you will be utterly reliant upon him, thus, you should be secure in the knowledge that he symbolises all that is possible in the advanced gundog.

Index